FEASTING ON ASPHALT

THE RIVER RUN

ALTON BROWN

Photos by Jean Claude Dhien

STEWART, TABORI & CHANG · NEW YORK

There are a lot of pictures in this book. The good ones, and I'm happy to say that's most of them, were taken by Jean Claude "J. C." Dhien, a Frenchman living in L.A. and a hell of a motorcyclist. On the first *Feasting* trip he would often pass me on his Triumph Speed Triple taking photos at the same time. He went through three back tires on that trip...bad boy.

The crew, from left to right, Bob Wooldridge, ride master, scout; Lamar Owen, cameraman; Mike Clark, audio recordist; Mark Apen, line producer; Bobby Earnhardt, lighting and coffee brewing; Brett Soll, image management; Brian "Bear" Lamar, transportation and production assistant; Ramon Engle, cameraman; and J. C.

A DANG FINE BUNCH OF FELLAS.

NOTEBOOK ENTRY

All of the selected log entries were recorded on site with an iPod fitted with a micro-phone. If the thoughts herein seem jostled, unorganized, ram-bling, or ridiculous, sorry. That's just how I talk. The note-book entries were taken directly from a now-mangled spiral-bound pad I kept with me at all times. I'm a big believer in record-ing thoughts while they're young, even if they're underdevel-oped. Oh, and these are only excerpts. The rest I'm saving for my memoirs.

FOR ME, FEASTING ON ASPHALT STARTED IN 1969. That was the year my parents had an opportunity to buy a small radio station not too far from the north Georgia town where they grew up. This might not have been such a shocking development had it not been for the fact that upon completion of their marriage vows they moved to southern California and made me. And there was no way I was moving to some hillbilly-infested, Appalachian backwater. Of course, when you're seven you don't have a lot of leverage, so one bright summer morning I found myself in the back of a Chrysler sedan with an aged Siamese cat and a coloring book.

We didn't have a ton of money, so our moving company consisted of a couple of U-Hauls driven by family friends. The trucks were so loaded down that they really couldn't manage freeway speeds, so we crept eastward on state and back roads, taking our time and stopping often to allow engines and brakes to cool. And to eat.

To their great credit, my folks could always smell a fake, and they made sure we kept to family-owned establishments whenever possible. Those are my favorite kinds of places now. To make a long story short, we pork-chopped, tamaled, apple-pied, blue-plate-speci-aled, spaghetti-dinnered, taco'd, barbecued, hamburgered, and tuna-casseroled ourselves across the country, and it turned out to be the best social studies lesson I've ever had because as the landscape changed so did the people and the food they cooked. And everywhere we went folks were happy to talk, to share their stories and listen to some of ours.

That summer we often ate with total strangers, folks we'd never seen before and most likely would never see again. To this day I believe that the most important food experience you can have, besides eating with your own family, is to break bread with strangers. There are few—if any—social acts that can provide so positive a spin on human interactions, and if we did more of it I feel certain there would be a lot less misery and misunderstanding on this planet.

Fast-forward forty years and road travel ain't what it used to be. Eisenhower's Autobahn (the interstate system), national food chains, and automobile manufacturers have taken us (quite willingly, it would seem) out of the realm of Kerouac and into the world of George Herbert's *Dune*, where drugged-up "Navigators" fold space and time without actually going anywhere. This didn't really bother me too much until my daughter reached the age I was in 1969. At this point she's already been robbed of any romantic notions about car travel. She's never lain on the back dash to watch the road flow out of the back of the car. No heads out of windows. She's never experienced that peculiar sensation of going to sleep in her bed only to awaken on a well-padded floorboard several hundred miles away. That's not because we haven't attempted the "transfer," but when you're dealing with a fifteen-point NASA-approved child seat, well, let's see you not wake up the "package." As for food, we're usually so busy getting where we're going that we stop at the very same fast-food drive-through when hunger strikes. The food is always exactly the same, and the only human contact is through those tiny speakers, some of which I understand now route directly to call centers in Delhi. As a result, my daughter is becoming one of the chicken-finger zombies who knows nothing of travel, only destinations.

When I voiced my concerns regarding this condition to contemporaries, they all said that they doubted any of the funky, old family joints still existed. And so I went to Food Network and presented an idea for launching a culi-cultural safari, an exploration into the present condition of American road food. They said "go," and in April 2006 my first team departed Isle of Palms, South Carolina, and made Los Angeles, California, four weeks later. The trip was marred by numerous problems, not the least of which was a disagreement with gravity that left me akimbo in a pile of Nevada gravel with a broken collarbone and a couple of busted ribs. After swearing never to attempt a journey like this again, I launched the second expedition from Venice, Louisiana, on April 19, 2007, in an attempt to locate the source of the Mississippi River and consume a large amount of fried food. These humble pages, amassed from various notebooks and journals, attempt to capture some of the flavor of said journey.

✦ ✦ ✦ ✦ ✦ ✦ ✦ ✦ ✦ ✦

A note on the recipes in this book: in some cases we were pleased to find folks willing to share their recipes. If that be the case, said recipe will bear the banner "Courtesy of..." If a recipe was provided, but required considerable adjustment to make it practical for the modern home cook, the banner reads, "Based on a recipe from..." If, as was true in most cases, the recipe was a jealously guarded secret, I have done my best to re-create the dish from scratch. If that be the case, the banner reads, "Inspired by..."

WHEREVER WE STOP, PEOPLE ALWAYS ASK, "WHAT'S WITH THE BIKES?" I hear that a lot, but there's not really an easy answer. For one thing, motorcycles are darned fun to ride. Even in rain or cold or bitter wind, I'd rather be on a bike than in any car on earth—even an Aston Martin DB9 Volante, and that's saying a lot. On a bike you are in the movie, not just watching it. You smell the mowed grass,

the stinky dead raccoon, the barbecue when it's still five miles away. You feel the sudden changes in road texture and air temperature, and when you lean deep into a corner, accelerating smoothly through and out on your intended line—dang. And there's something zen-like about the kind of attention you have to pay when you're on a bike. You can stare into the middle distance, but your attention can never wander far from what you're doing or you'll end up in a ditch, or worse. (Of course, that can happen even when you're paying attention if there are bunnies in the vicinity.)

But most of all, I like traveling by bike because motorcycles are wonderful icebreakers. It's amazing to me how many times we can pull up at a place and immediately people want to talk to us, not about food, but about the bikes. I don't think it's because of the bikes themselves so much as what they represent: freedom, adventure, a touch of danger, perhaps. But regardless of where we stop, the second our helmets are off someone's asking where we've been and where we're going and how far and how much rain and, gee, do you like that BMW and how's your mileage and then there's my favorite: are you hungry? People are also less likely to recognize a food quasi-celebrity like me if I've got a nasty case of helmet hair and five days of growth...and a funny smell. So, it's kinda like a disguise (guess that's why Brad Pitt rides, too).

ALTHOUGH I TACKLED THE FIRST FEAST-
ING ON A BMW R1200RT SPORT TOUR BIKE,
I'VE LEARNED MY LESSON ABOUT THE CHAL-
LENGES OF SHIFTING TERRAIN AND HAVE
CHOSEN THIS TIME TO TRAVEL UPON A BMW
R1200GS, WHICH IS MADE FOR MORE AGGRES-
SIVE OFF-ROAD PURSUITS WHILE STILL BEING
COMFORTABLE FOR HOURS ON ASPHALT. WITH
A GOOD GPS AND SOME HARD SIDE BAGS AND
TOP BOX, I'D BE WILLING TO TAKE THIS BIKE
ANYWHERE ON THE PLANET. I CHOSE YELLOW,
AND I'M GLAD I DID BECAUSE NOW I CAN
NAME THE BIG MULE BUTTERCUP, AFTER
DALE EVANS'S HORSE.

ACTUALLY, EVERYONE ON THIS TRIP
BROUGHT A GS ALONG. BOB, BEING A BIG
GUY, IS RIDING THE GS ADVENTURE,
WHICH SITS CONSIDERABLY HIGHER, FEA-
TURES MORE CRASH-PROOFING, AND HAS
A BIGGER GAS TANK. NICE...BUT TOO
BIG FOR ME. BUTTERCUP'S JUST RIGHT.
GIDDY-YUP, GIRL.

DRIVE THRU

Hot from the kitchen
- PEELED SHRIMP
- STUFFED ARTICHOKES
- MANUEL'S HOT TAMALES
- CHICKEN AND GUMBO
- SHRIMP & OKRA GUMBO
- JAMBALAYA •• RABBITS
- SMOTHERED OKRA

Greetings from LOUISIANA

State Flower
the Magnolia

State Capitol
in Baton Rouge

MISSISSIPPI

LOUISIANA

mden
El Dorado
Greenville
Yazoo City
Vicksburg
JACKSON
20
Minden
Monroe
Natchitoches
Lorman
Brookhaven
49
Natchez
59
McComb
ineville
Bogalusa
Red R.
55
Morganza
St. Francisville
Abita Springs
BATON ROUGE
Plaquemine
Gulfport
10
Laplace
Hammond
Donaldsonville
New Orleans
Lafayette
Vacherie
Belle Chasse
Point A La Hache
Buras
Galliano
Venice
Gulf of Mexico

Luzianne Tea

A STRONG BROWN GOD

PERSONS | DATE | CHECK NO. | AMOUNT

8624- 1

DAY ONE
PLAQUEMINES PARISH,
LOUISIANA
0800 HOURS

WELCOME
YOU HAVE REACHED THE
SOUTHERNMOST POINT
IN LOUISIANA
GATEWAY TO THE GU

I've never visited a geography like this before, a kaleidoscope of land and water that makes not one bit of sense. Like God turned on a thousand garden hoses and just let them flop around the yard like a big, lazy hydra.

The sign says this is the end of the road, and it's not kidding. A quarter mile of straight-shot tarmac, a couple feet of gravel, a clump of weeds, then water. Standing here I can't help but wonder, if I took that quarter mile wide open, how much space could I clear before splashdown? Tempting but off-mission.

Evidence of the storm is everywhere—chunks of boats, bits of oil derrick, countless pieces of what were once useful things slowly swallowed by the bayou like a pig by a python. Given a few years the hydra will forget the whole thing.

We set up our map for the first shot of the journey. I try not to think about what I'll say, because I believe that there are few things more honest than just stepping in front of a camera and going. On my other projects I write everything ahead. On this, I haven't. Sometimes that's a good thing. Sometimes not.

I babble about Mark Twain, who wrote that "the Mississippi will always have its own way," and T. S. Eliot, who called the river "a strong brown god."

I recount our mission statement: eat our way up the river, avoid freeways, chains, and all forms of whining, documenting all—the good, the bad, even the untasty.

Before departing this wild confusion I want to see Head of Passes, the glove-shaped split of the main navigable channel that is the datum from which all distances on the lower river are measured. The main fingers, the Southwest Pass, the Pass-a-Loutre (otter's pass), and the South Pass, are easily seen from space and helicopter.

Down here helicopters are everywhere, their drone a constant reminder of the oil derricks working out in the gulf. We hire a bug-like Robinson 44 out of Jesuit Bend about fifty miles up Highway 23 from Venice and find it parked on a pad behind a barn surrounded by horses, who barely notice when we take off. Skimming the water, we move around countless barges, tankers, and container ships moving goods up and down the river. No one knows how many pounds of paper, iron, chemicals, wheat, corn, and oil find their way to market every day along its roughly 2320 navigable miles, but guesses are in the billions of tons a year. That's a lot. And it's still one of the most economical methods of transportation, which explains why more than a few big thinkers have pointed out that America

BELOW: Flying out to Head Of Passes, where the Mississippi meets the Gulf of Mexico. You can see empty barges tied up on the bank...waiting for whatever.

14

> *I've run less risk driving my way across country than eating my way across it.*
> DUNCAN HINES

wouldn't have become America without the Mississippi. I'm also struck by how many FEMA trailers we see. They're everywhere, housing people whose lives were wiped out and away by wind and sea.

✦ ✦ ✦ ✦ ✦ ✦ ✦ ✦ ✦ ✦

There is precious little to eat in this neck of the woods, so we motor north toward New Orleans. I haven't been back since Katrina and I'm a bit apprehensive. I've made arrangements for only one stop in these parts, the Luzianne Tea factory. I'm a huge fan of iced tea, Luzianne tea in particular, and the factory managers have been nice enough to let us have a look around. Pulling into the lot, there is little evidence that just twenty months ago it was in six feet of water. When the marauding river finally retreated, the parking lot was left holding thousands of dead, stinking eels. Yum.

BELOW: Imagine this scene covering an area the size of Connecticut and you start to get an idea of what the land is like down here.

15

ALTHOUGH ICED TEA HAD BEEN CONSUMED IN THE SOUTH FOR AT LEAST A CENTURY, THE BEVERAGE GOT ITS FIRST BIG MARKETING PUSH WHEN IT WAS SERVED AT THE 1904 WORLD'S FAIR IN ST. LOUIS.

We're led through the warehouses where teas are brought from all over the world for blending, a job managed by a giant mixer fed by overhead grates. It's a relatively simple job until you take into account that tea is an agricultural product with characteristics that are constantly in flux. Keeping the brand's flavor on target requires constant toil.

The room where the tea bags are made, filled, and packaged would make Willy Wonka blush. Gears whirl and cogs spin and little mechanical arms do whatever they're programmed to do. There are no computers in evidence, and I'm told that most of the machines are as old as I am. It's nice to know they're still working.

I receive a lesson in tea cupping from Malcolm Shalders, who is Luzianne's head flavor enforcer. I slurp from a dozen or so cups, spitting each mouthful into a dentist's-office spit basin, and understand almost nothing. It's hard to make good iced tea. Just leave it at that.

✦ ✦ ✦ ✦ ✦ ✦ ✦ ✦ ✦ ✦

NEW ORLEANS, LOUISIANA
NIGHTFALL

It is perhaps not a smart thing to enter a major city to shoot a food show with no idea of where you're going to eat, especially when you're a bunch of hungry guys on motorcycles being clumsily shadowed by a thirty-six-foot motor home. (It took Bear a few days to figure out he'd been hogging both lanes.)

Anyway, I know I want to stay clear of the Quarter, because that seems to be where all the TV people go. I'm afraid that everything there was tourist before and now it's even more tourist. We end up in the Warehouse District in front of a classic local spot called Mulate's. I go in and check it out. Big place. Great smells, zippy zydeco, a hundred hungry tourists. Loud. Way too loud for shooting. Too bad—the gumbo looks good.

I leave Mulate's and start making phone calls, trying to find sustenance for my guys. I pick up a few leads on the street but have no luck. Everything's mysteriously closed. Meanwhile, a small and friendly crowd has gathered. Someone asks if Rachael Ray is there, and I say no because there wasn't anywhere to land the jet. Finally I give up and call for card tables to be brought forth. We will feast on the street… on asphalt. After some begging, a waiter who happens to be a *Good Eats* fan (smart lad) agrees to serve both food and beverage to us in our makeshift dining room. (It should be noted that our policy is no beer for bikers until the day's ride is done. This does not keep any of the rest of

OPPOSITE: **Gotta love old school tech. This tea bag filler was made the same year I was. And it works a lot harder.** OPPOSITE INSET: **Cupping tea in the Luzianne tasting room.**

NOTEBOOK ENTRY

Luzianne was founded by William B. Reily in the 1870s. Back then coffee was the company focus (they still make a fine chicory coffee), but as refrigeration and ice became more common, Southerners started drinking more and more iced tea. Sensing a trend, Reily decided to come up with a blend of teas just for icing.

the crew from imbibing several Abita Turbodogs.) I stick to iced tea that is not sweetened in any way, fashion, or form. When I inquire about this to a passerby, she informs me that New Orleans tea is never sweetened. Mon Dieu!

Food starts pouring onto our rickety buffet. Alligator, gumbos, étouffées, sausages, tasty little meat pies, rice and beans...and it's all good. Very good. Some of the musicians wander out and serenade us, passersby ask for tastes, which we give out generously until the bread pudding comes. Then all bets are off. It is creamy and dense and oddly uniform for a dessert known for its hunks-and-chunks texture. Turns out they make it from leftover hamburger buns, which they soak in eggs and cream until the buns lose all form and shape. With hard sauce, the pudding's amazing. (I'm sure all the alcohol was cooked out. That's my story, at least.) We're visited by one of the Mulate family, who runs the place. He tries his best to pick up the check, but we resist and threaten to start rumors of foodborne illness. He relents, but I still don't think the check reflected the considerable damage done by my crew.

BELOW: Wilson Touchet, John Deloney, and Gilbert Giroir serenade us outside Mulate's.

One of the most unusual bread puddings I've sampled. The texture is smooth and dense, with no real evidence of the bread at all. It actually reminds me of a tres leches cake—and that's a good thing.

MULATE'S HOMEMADE BREAD PUDDING
COURTESY OF MULATE'S
NEW ORLEANS, LOUISIANA

+ +

- 6 large eggs
- 2 cups whole milk
- 2 cups half-and-half
- 1 cup sugar
- 1 teaspoon vanilla extract
- 6 hamburger buns
- ½ cup raisins
- Butter or nonstick spray for the pan

Preheat the oven to 350 degrees. Grease a 9-by-13-inch pan and set aside.

In a large mixing bowl, whisk the eggs. Add the milk, half-and-half, sugar, and vanilla and whisk well to combine.

Break the hamburger buns into pieces and place in the prepared pan. Sprinkle the raisins evenly over the buns and pour the liquid mixture over. Make sure that all of the bread is thoroughly soaked in the liquid. Bake on the middle rack of the oven for 45 minutes. Let cool for 15 minutes before serving. If you prefer a firmer texture, chill for about 2 hours, then reheat for serving.

YIELD: 10 TO 12 SERVINGS

BUTTER RUM SAUCE

+ +

- 4 tablespoons (½ stick) unsalted butter
- ¼ cup sugar
- ½ cup heavy cream
- ½ cup rum*

Place the butter in a 1-quart saucepan and set over medium heat. Once the butter has melted, add the sugar and whisk to combine. Cook for 3 minutes. Add the cream and rum and cook for 5 minutes, or until slightly thickened. Serve warm over the bread pudding.

*Although you can use any rum you want, I rely on a dark spiced rum for this.

TOP: Tommy McConnell, our curbside waiter. Truth be told, i think he liked getting out of the madness inside.
ABOVE: Mulate's bread pudding is amazingly uniform and creamy, yet dense. And they were willing to share the recipe.

✦ ✦ ✦ ✦ ✦ ✦ ✦ ✦ ✦ ✦

DAY TWO
FRENCH QUARTER
0500 HOURS

I can't sleep, so I'm in the world-famous Café du Monde trying to balance mouthfuls of beignets, buried in powdered sugar, with sips of hot chicory coffee.

The roots of chicory (*Cichorium intybus*), a form of endive, have been used as a vegetable for thousands of years, but when revolutions in Santo Domingo and Haiti at the beginning of the nineteenth century cut off a major portion of France's coffee bean supply, roasted chicory was used to flesh out the supply. For some, especially those living in Louisiana, coffee just isn't coffee without chicory. There aren't too many American roasters still working with chicory, but a stroll around the web will flush them out pretty quickly.

Part of me knows that this is a gimmicky place. Heck, the beignets aren't even any good, and I don't know a single local who eats here. And yet no one can argue that Café du Monde isn't authentic. That's because it is indelibly connected to this place and to its culture. You might argue that if that is the definition of authentic, then McDonald's must represent authentic American cuisine. I would counter that had McDonald's stuck to southern California the way, say, In-and-Out Burger has (with one exception, I know: Vegas), it would be authentic. By spreading out beyond its natural geocultural borders, a chain sacrifices its authenticity. Since I can think of no exceptions, I'm going to call this a rule.

I finish my third beignet wishing I'd stopped at two and walk over to the river to watch the sunrise across the big crescent. This is the first spot I've encountered where there is no levee to climb. That's because the French Quarter is the high ground of New Orleans. It has not always been a pleasant place. The geologist brothers Kolb and Van Topik referred to the site as "a land between earth and sea belonging to neither and alternately claimed by both." Repeated cycles of flooding have built up the land on the outside of the big curve where the quarter sits. This is why there is literally no evidence of Katrina's wrath here while many of the other districts are still in ruins. A shame in the richest country in the world, if you ask me.

RIGHT: Morning in the French Quarter. Where the heck is everybody?
OPPOSITE INSET: The second stop of the day—ice cream.

✦ ✦ ✦ ✦ ✦ ✦ ✦ ✦ ✦ ✦

MAGAZINE ST.
1000 HOURS

I have no idea where we're going as we head out for the day, but we end up on Magazine Street and that's a good thing because by 10 a.m. a biker yearns for gelato. La Davina, owned and operated by Carmelo Turillo and his wife, Katrina (a tough tag to tow in these

parts), opened just weeks before the storm. It's back now and going strong, one of the new businesses that seem to be rising from the city's sodden ashes. The gelatos, each of which is made from its own base (most gelato americano is made from a single base—more economic, don't ya know), are amazing. The strawberry-black pepper-balsamic gelato is my favorite. And the espresso's good, though there's no chicory. We saunter up and down the street to work up additional appetite, and that's when I run into a couple of line cooks from Commander's Palace. I ask them about landing some crawfish, and they suggest a place a couple of blocks on up the street called Big Fisherman Seafood.

✦ ✦ ✦ ✦ ✦ ✦ ✦ ✦ ✦ ✦

OPPOSITE: Craw-fish, aka mud bugs, aka crawdads—like lobster, only smaller, meaner, and better-tasting. BOTTOM: Henry Poynot, the Big Fisherman himself.

Big Fisherman Seafood is a nondescript stucco building on the corner of Magazine and Toledano. I go in and find a small, humble shop. Everything is local, from redfish to bins of shrimp to bushels of crawfish. Peeking through the hallway to the back, I can see the giant gas-powered boilers working away and huge bags of twitching mud bugs awaiting their fate. My mouth waters.

I inquire as to the whereabouts of the owner, and of course he's right there. The good owners always are my friends. His name is Henry Poynot and he's been fishing professionally since he was twelve. Henry's very fit, an Iron Man triathlete, and deeply intelligent. His voice is deeply accented and it takes me a while to get used to it. Henry ended up with this place because he used to sell the shrimp he caught to the previous owner. When one of the owner's checks bounced, Henry came over to take care of things. He found the business closed and the bum gone. Henry found out who owned the building and asked if he could take over the lease. Now Henry's one of the last true independents left, a real bridge between fishermen and the local population, which is very loyal.

Henry takes me to the back, where forty to fifty pounds of bugs boil at a time, in water thoroughly seasoned by Henry's special boil mix, the composition of which is of course a complete secret. (Extracting recipes out of Southerners is pretty near impossible.)

The rest of the crew shows up and, being a good host, Henry insists we eat. There are no tables in the store, but by the front window there's a big freezer for shrimp. We cover the freezer with newspaper while Henry fills a bin with fresh crawfish, corn, potatoes, garlic, and sausage. He then dumps the contents onto the freezer along with some stuffed and baked artichokes (a local delicacy that I still haven't been able to find origins for).

Henry gives lessons on how to eat crawfish, and I discover that I've been doing it wrong all these years. You have to push the tail in before you twist and pull. That way you get the maximum

tail meat. You then grasp the tail in your palm so that you can press the top of your thumb against the underside of the tail, where there's no armor to speak of. Then you just flick your thumb upwards to extract the meat. It's easier than it sounds, but not by much if you're a novice. Then there's the issue of head-sucking, which requires biting down and sucking down hard while twisting your own head up and to the side at the same time, lest messiness issue down the front of your riding jacket. It's a complicated business, and completely worth it. And no, this isn't the same as eating brains, because crawfish have no brains to speak of. It's more like slurping out all the internal organs, which on paper doesn't really seem any more appetizing than sucking out a brain, does it?

Before leaving the Big Fisherman I ask about the water bags. Each door is flanked by a hanging clear plastic bag, half full of water with a penny in the bottom. Turns out these are very effective fly repellents. It has something to do with the way fly vision works: scares them away or confuses them or maybe it's just plain voodoo. I'll have to do some experimentation to figure this one out. I do notice, however, that there are no flies in any part of the Big Fisherman, front or back.

I point out to Henry as we leave that although I am beyond grateful for the Big Easy welcome he gave to us suddenly appearing strangers, I'm a little disappointed that our fete was sans alligator. He smiles and says that if I want to know about alligator I've got to go visit this fella's alligator farm out on the other side of Lake Pontchartrain. Not exactly on our way, but what the heck. I'll bite.

OPPOSITE TOP:
Crawfish boil in a secret spice mix—50 pounds at a time.
OPPOSITE BOTTOM:
NASA has nothing on the Big Fisherman.

NOTEBOOK ENTRY

many folks are confused about the meanings of cajun and creole where food is concerned. Although they both have deep French roots, creole is more genteel, cosmopolitan if you will. It calls for a fair amount of butter, butter rouxs, and many tomatoes. It is seasoned in a European sense, which is to say not very much

at all. Étouffée is a typical edible representative of creole cuisine. cajun, on the other hand, rarely calls for butter or tomatoes. Seasoning is high, with plenty of cayenne and spicy, cured meats. Thickening is done with dark rouxs. Gumbo would be a darned good representative, along with andouille sausage and tasso.

ABOVE: **There are no tables at Big Fisherman Seafood so we spread newspapers on top of the big freezer.**

I just don't think it's right to call it a "crawfish boil" unless you have at least fifteen pounds of bugs, but if you want to be skimpy, obviously you can cut this recipe down. If you can't get your hands on Big Fisherman boil mix, use any boil mix you can find and add a pinch—make that a big pinch—of cayenne.

CRAWFISH BOIL

COURTESY OF BIG FISHERMAN SEAFOOD
NEW ORLEANS, LOUISIANA

✦ ✦ ✦ ✦ ✦ ✦ ✦ ✦ ✦ ✦ ✦ ✦ ✦ ✦ ✦ ✦

**15 pounds crawfish
2 pounds kosher salt, divided
4 gallons water
3½ ounces Big Fisherman Seafood boil mix*
5 tablespoons Chinese pepper (a Cajun pepper blend)*
2 pounds small new potatoes
6 ears corn, cut in half
2 heads garlic, unpeeled**

Place the crawfish in a large bowl of cool water and add half of the salt. Stir around until the mud and dirt come off the crawfish. Rinse and pick out any debris and dead crawfish. Rinse several times with fresh water until the water runs clear, 8 to 10 times.

Fill an 8-gallon pot with the water and add the rest of the salt, the boil mix, and the Chinese pepper. Bring to a boil over high heat and stir to combine. Once the mixture comes to a boil, add the potatoes, corn, and garlic. Cook for 10 minutes.

Add the crawfish and boil for 3 minutes. Remove from the heat and let soak for 10 minutes to allow the crawfish and vegetables to absorb the flavors. Drain and serve.

* See the list of sources on page 202 to purchase.

YIELD: 6 TO 8 SERVINGS

The first condition of understanding a foreign country is to smell it.
RUDYARD KIPLING

I have not been able to find a reliable source that explains how artichokes became associated with Cajun cuisine. But they're pretty tasty regardless.

STUFFED ARTICHOKES
COURTESY OF BIG FISHERMAN SEAFOOD
NEW ORLEANS, LOUISIANA

+ +

2 cups seasoned bread crumbs

2 cups shredded Parmesan cheese

⅓ cup garlic powder

¼ cup dried parsley

2 teaspoons kosher salt, divided

¼ teaspoon freshly ground black pepper

½ cup olive oil

¼ cup water

4 whole artichokes

2 tablespoons freshly squeezed lemon juice

4 lemon slices

½ teaspoon paprika

Preheat oven to 340 degrees. In a large bowl, combine the bread crumbs, cheese, garlic powder, parsley, 1 teaspoon of the salt, and the pepper. Add the oil and water and stir to combine. The mixture should be moist and loose. Set the filling aside.

Trim the tops of the artichokes by about 3 inches. Trim off the stems, and trim the tips of any remaining leaves. Place the artichokes in an 8-quart pot and cover with water. (The artichokes will float.) Add the remaining 1 teaspoon salt and the lemon juice to the water. Bring to a boil, cover, and cook until tender, 20 to 25 minutes.

Remove the artichokes from the water and let them cool upside down. Once they are cool to the touch, squeeze any remaining water out. Scoop out the middle to remove the fuzzy choke. Slightly push the leaves apart.

Place the artichokes in a 9-by-13-inch glass baking dish. Evenly divide the filling among the artichokes, making sure to get some in between the leaves. Top with the lemon slices and sprinkle with the paprika. Pour just enough water in the dish to cover the bottom of the artichokes. Cover with foil and bake for 25 minutes. Remove the foil and continue baking for another 10 minutes. Let cool slightly before serving.

YIELD: 4 SERVINGS

ABOVE: The fact that artichokes don't grow anywhere around these parts doesn't mean that stuffed and baked artichokes can't be a local favorite.

✦ ✦ ✦ ✦ ✦ ✦ ✦ ✦ ✦ ✦

KLIEBERT'S TURTLE & ALLIGATOR TOURS, HAMMOND, LOUISIANA
1550 HOURS

I'm standing on a small concrete ramp that juts abruptly into a swampy pond covered with assorted floating plant life. And I'm thinking about lawyers. I'm thinking about how lawyers would never allow me to be where I am right now. Especially without the proprietor, Mr. Kliebert, a gentleman in his sixties in camouflage overalls, who has disappeared in his pickup truck, leaving me here. Inside the fence. With them.

Them being *Alligator mississippiensis*, or American alligators. The big males are twelve to fourteen feet long, while the females are relatively petite and little more than six feet long. There seem to be hundreds of them in this primitive place, but I'm mostly concerned with the five or six that are coming my way in search of a meal. When the first of the beasts scrapes and pulls his prehistoric, scaly self up onto the ramp, I think about the fact that more people in this country have been killed by gators in this millennium than in all other recorded years combined. And although the alligators seem stupid and slow, I also think about the fact that in short bursts they can hit fifty miles an hour.

None of us have ever been this close to wild gators before, and we're not used to the funny (okay, more scary than funny) sounds they make, which range from sighs to long, low growls. Then there's the sound of claws on con-

ABOVE: **A 10 footer helps himself to a nutria head.**
OPPOSITE: **Mr. Kliebert and friend.**

NOTEBOOK ENTRY

Nutrias, or Nyocastor coypus, are semiaquatic rodents of remarkable size. Natives of South America, they were imported here in the 1930s for their fur. (Apparently in Russia, nutria fur is quite the rage.) Of course, importing animals is rarely a good idea, because they always get out

and wreak havoc, and that's just what the nutria have done, mowing through wetland vegetation. By using them for gator bait, Mr. Kliebert is doing everyone a favor, except perhaps the nutria, who currently have not gained the support of PETA or any other animal rights lobbying group, as far as I can tell.

crete. The hair on my neck stands up. This Jurassic thing is about five feet away from me and between us is nothing but humid, mosquito-saturated air. Luckily, before I can reach my phone and consult my lawyer, Kliebert returns with a big bin of frozen nutria parts.

Kliebert coaches me on the fine art of feeding gators without becoming a snack yourself. He explains that they're just coming out of hibernation so they're a tad slow. Good. Kliebert has coaxed one right up to him, and it's a big guy, probably fifty years old. He's making even scarier sounds than the others, and when he crunches down on the first nutria snack, it's pure T-rex. I'm now at the water with one of the big males about two feet away, and his head is some eighteen inches across, I guess, and a good two feet from muzzle to tonsil. I get in a nutria head and just as the crush comes I reach out and touch the gator on the nose. Then I jump back with a speed that surprises everyone—not least myself. As I get more used to the idea that I'm probably not going to be devoured I start to question Kliebert. His family practically invented alligator farming, and it's an industry that's actually appreciated by conservationist groups. Indeed, management techniques

BELOW: Generally speaking, if there's a crowd of men and one of them does something stupid, others will soon rise up to copy him. Here, it's my turn to pet the dinosaur. And no, they are not tame in any way, shape, or form.

used by alligator farmers are in no small part responsible for the gator's removal from the endangered animal list back in 1987. As for the harvested goods, much of the meat is sold but now that it's open season on hides, the luxury leather industry can't get enough.

Alligator meat is harvested mostly from the tail, and it's a tough job because the lean stuff is layered in with fat and must be "stripped out" to be edible. Although I've heard some folks say that alligator tastes like chicken, it doesn't. It only "tastes" that way because it's most often served in fried strips that look like chicken fingers. I'd much rather have it sautéed.

Kliebert asks me if I want to catch one. I'm a guy. Of course I want to catch one. He leads me to another pen with another, smaller pond. A bunch of three- and four-footers are hanging around. He grabs one by the tail, then just behind the head, and stands there with it. I do the same, and it's like trying to hold on to a big bundle of solid muscle, which is pretty much what an alligator is. After a couple of tries I get the hang of it but decide not to challenge myself with the parents.

Sourcing your tail will be the toughest part of preparing this toothsome treat. Check the sources list on page 202 for a couple of suggestions.

GRILLED ALLIGATOR TAIL WITH LEMON AND GARLIC BUTTER
COURTESY OF KLIEBERT'S TURTLE & ALLIGATOR TOURS, INC.
HAMMOND, LOUISIANA

✦ ✦ ✦ ✦ ✦ ✦ ✦ ✦ ✦ ✦ ✦ ✦ ✦ ✦ ✦ ✦ ✦ ✦ ✦

2 pounds alligator tail meat
4 ounces (1 stick) unsalted butter
½ clove garlic, minced
½ cup freshly squeezed lemon juice

BELOW: This is either an example of what happens when a small boy puts on a gator head that's too big for him, or what happens when gator cousins marry.
OPPOSITE: How wonderful, your dinner comes with a bonus belt and wallet.

Preheat a charcoal grill to medium.

In a small microwaveable bowl, melt the butter. Add the garlic and lemon juice. Using a silicon pastry brush, coat the alligator with the butter mixture. Place the alligator on the grill. Turn and baste the alligator with the butter mixture every 5 to 7 minutes until done, about 20 minutes. Serve hot.

YIELD: 4 SERVINGS

NOTEBOOK ENTRY

So, who first thought to serve up this toothy Saurian? Seems native American tribes from South Carolina to Louisiana have been noshing gator since prehistory. The French trader Jacques Le Moyne de Morgue wrote in 1591 of Florida natives smoking alligator for winter consumption. The tails of young specimens were preferred, as adults were deemed too gamey (not to mention too toothy).

Southern consumption was later boosted by slaves who had eaten both the flesh and the fat of the crocodile in Africa, quite possibly as a preemptive measure against being consumed themselves. The closest thing to an actual gator celebrity endorsement I can find is a quote from the famed naturalist and painter John James Audubon, who wrote in 1837, "alligator flesh is far from being bad." How's that for a sell line?

After playing about with dinosaurs for most of the afternoon, we are hungry to dine upon their succulence. Although Kliebert doesn't actually serve any gator, he knows where to send us.

✦ ✦ ✦ ✦ ✦ ✦ ✦ ✦ ✦ ✦

B&C SEAFOOD, HIGHWAY 18, VACHERIE, LOUISIANA
1923 HOURS

Highway 18 winds along the southern bank of the Mississippi from Paulina to Vacherie and there, right next to the levee, is B&C Seafood market and Cajun restaurant. With a restaurant on one side and a market featuring smoked and cured goodies processed on the premises, this is my kind of place. B&C is chock-full of alligator paraphernalia including, but not limited to, various taxidermied gators posed in strange, humanoid positions, some of which give me a case of the freesons (that's Cajun for goosebumps). After ordering just about everything on the menu from gumbo to boudin balls, beans and rice to alligator four ways, we wander into the shop side and buy up bags of cracklins (fried pork skin) and filé powder in tiny jars bearing the name of Lionel Key, Baton Rouge, Louisiana. This makes me right curious, seeing as how we're planning on passing through the capital in the next couple of days.

 The food at B&C is way above average and the tea is first class, thanks to the inclusion of just a spoonful of sugar somewhere along the line. But the real marvel, to me at least, is the zydeco salad. Maybe it's because my system is starved for anything green, but at this moment I cannot stop eating it. The olive salad and the canned beans manage to marry into the lettuce and tomatoes. And on the platter it looks like a party. I ask about the name, assuming that in this case "zydeco," the creole/Cajun music form based on lots of syncopated accordion, was simply a colorful marketing term. Mais non, cher. "Zydeco" comes from "les haricots sont pas salés," which means "the beans aren't salty," an expression for hard times when there wasn't enough salt meat to season the beans. So this salad, with its three different beans, is actually zydeco and the musical genre is named after it. I told you food was fascinating stuff.

BELOW: Like so many other cooks we encountered in the south, Sandra Dabney has been cooking all her life.

Take

this to your next covered-dish dinner or picnic. Finding the Italian olive salad—the chopped-olive spread that's an essential component of a muffaletta sandwich—is the trick. If you can't find it at the megamart it's easily found on the web.

ZYDECO SALAD

COURTESY OF B&C SEAFOOD
VACHERIE, LOUISIANA

✦ ✦

4 cups shredded iceberg lettuce
2 medium tomatoes
1 (15-ounce) can three-bean salad, drained
8 ounces Italian olive salad

Place the lettuce on a platter or serving dish. Top with the tomatoes, then the olive salad, then the three-bean salad. Serve immediately.

YIELD: 6 TO 8 SERVINGS

BELOW LEFT: Oddly enough my favorite dish at B&C was this unusual "zydeco" salad composed of various lettuces, the olive relish made for muffaletta sandwiches, and canned three-bean salad. Odd, but delicious… maybe I needed vegetables worse than I thought.
BELOW RIGHT: The store side of B&C. Local delicacies and more gators.

◆　◆　◆　◆　◆　◆　◆　◆　◆

DAY THREE
BAILEY'S ANDOUILLE & PRODUCE, LAPLACE, LOUISIANA
1030 HOURS

Today's highlight is definitely Bailey's Andouille & Produce in Laplace. Nondescript and tucked into the end of a suburban-style strip mall, what catches my eye is the big, hand-made sign picturing an andouille sausage come to life. The thing has to be twenty feet tall at least. We swing in, unannounced as usual. Within moments Mr. Bailey, a distinguished-looking Cajun in his early sixties, pokes out his head and suspiciously eyes our invasion. Then he sees the bikes and his eyes light up. He starts telling me about this old Triumph he had back in the day and that we need to come in and check out the sausage. Turns out Ernest Bailey Sr. has just turned the operation of the store and all sausage processing over to his son, an erstwhile accountant.

> Oh public road, you express me better than I can express myself.
> WALT WHITMAN

Both of the Bailey men are talkers, and as we check out their refrig-erated cases and the walls covered with award citations for excellence in sausage making, it's clear that there's plenty to talk about. I ask how it's possible that this store isn't packed to the gills all day every day. Both men shrug and point to the traffic outside, four lanes with a center turn lane that's tough to negotiate, and a very funky light half a block down that complicates things. It's that exact moment, as I'm craning my neck to see the traf-fic, that I see the suit in the corner. A custom-made, full-size, sports team mascot–style sausage suit. Since he's done this sort of work on *Good Eats* before, I immediately sum-mon Brett, who despite the heat hesitates not a moment when he hears his assignment. He dons the smoky mantle and we head out to dance in the street, or rather next to it. Working the curb like pros, Brett dances like a fool while I chant witty slogans like "How can you people let your great food traditions die out, you morons?" And "Hey, you, get your sausage here!" And "You deserve a smoky tube of pork today!" Amazingly, some drivers respond and pull in to check the place out. But the effort has taken its toll on Brett, who is nearing heat exhaustion. We decide to go in for root beer and food.

NOTEBOOK ENTRY

Andouille sausage: a coarse smoked sau-sage composed of pork, sometimes chitterlings, pep-per, garlic, and seasonings. Although French in origin, it is mostly associated with cajun cooking, especially as a sea-soning element for gumbo.

ME AND MR. ANDOUILLE
STRIKE A POSE FOR FLAVOR.
(THE FACT THAT THE
CHARACTER ON THE SIGN
CLOSELY RESEMBLES A
CHARACTER FROM SOUTH
PARK MAY NOT WORK IN THE
BAILEYS FAVOR.)

Safely ensconced in air-conditioned comfort, we hungrily sample an assortment of sausages, each with a perfect balance of spice and smoke, not too little of one or too much of the other. And great googly moogly, there's head cheese. Now, let me start by saying that head cheese has absolutely nothing to do with cheese and everything to do with head—or at least it used to. These days Mr. Bailey says that the FDA or USDA or whoever won't allow them to use head at all, so they make a spicy stock and add lean shoulder meat. I ask him what the world is coming to and his head kinda drops. He doesn't know what the world is coming to either. We shrug off the mystery and dig into the gumbo (damned fine), buy half a ton of pork products, and move on, having gotten some great stories from a great family of Cajun cuisine.

This stuff is great on crackers, it's true, but if you really want to let the stuff out, melt it over grits.

HOG'S HEAD CHEESE
INSPIRED BY BAILEY'S ANDOUILLE & PRODUCE
LAPLACE, LOUISIANA

✦ ✦

> 3 to 4 pounds Boston butt, trimmed and cut into 1- to 1½-inch pieces
> 2 smoked ham hocks
> 2 quarts water
> 5 (¼-ounce) packages unflavored gelatin
> 1 tablespoon plus 2 teaspoons kosher salt
> 2 teaspoons freshly ground black pepper
> 1½ teaspoons garlic powder
> 2 teaspoons paprika
> 1 teaspoon red pepper flakes

Place the meat and ham hocks in a 6-quart stockpot and add the water. Bring to a boil over high heat. Lower the heat in order to maintain a low boil and cook, uncovered, until the meat is tender, about 1 hour. The water should have decreased to 1 quart. Add or pour off enough water to make 1 quart.

Remove the meat and ham hocks from the pot. Discard the ham hocks. Place the meat in a separate container and store in the refrigerator. Place the pot of cooking water in the refrigerator, uncovered, and let cool completely, 2 to 3 hours. Once cooled, remove the fat cap that has formed. When cool enough to handle, shred three quarters of the meat, chop the remaining meat into ¼-inch cubes, and store in the refrigerator until ready to use.

Place the gelatin in a small bowl and pour 1 cup of the liquid from the pot over the gelatin. Set aside. Return the meat to the pot and add the salt, black pepper, garlic powder, paprika, and red pepper flakes and stir to combine. Place over high heat and bring to a heavy rolling boil, 6 to 8 minutes. Remove from the heat and stir in the gelatin mixture. Pour the mixture into a 9-by-5-inch loaf pan and set in the refrigerator overnight. Slice and serve as an appetizer or add to grits for a hearty breakfast.

YIELD: 10 TO 12 SERVINGS

NOTEBOOK ENTRY

To make traditional head cheese you kill a pig and saw off its head, which you then clean of all hair and anything else that might not already be considered repulsive seeing as how you just cut off a pig's head. Then you boil the head with various seasonings until all the meat balls off and a majority of the connective tissue dissolves. (It's like making stock, only you're after meat and gelatin.) You pull out

✦ ✦ ✦ ✦ ✦ ✦ ✦ ✦ ✦

ST. JOSEPH'S PLANTATION, VACHERIE, LOUISIANA
1438 HOURS

I'm standing in one of the front rooms of St. Joseph's Plantation looking at a map drawn up some twenty years before the Civil War showing all the plantations in Louisiana. Up to this moment I had not realized that they lined up like condos on the beach, in some cases less than a hundred feet from the river. This of course makes sense. Plantations capable of moving goods and crops by riverboat would have a serious edge on road-bound commerce. Having plantations butted up against each other would also make it harder for runaway slaves to make much progress.

St. Joseph's has been in the Boudreaux family for 130 years. Joan Boudreaux shows me around her amazingly well-preserved house. The portrait she paints of plantation life is decidedly un–*Gone with the Wind*-like. Life was hard and everyone worked long hours, whether in the "big house" or in the fields. For many slaves and their owners, the Emancipation Proclamation didn't change much. Slaves had nowhere to go, and planters

BELOW: **Joan Boudreaux, the current family proprietress of St. Joseph's.**

the stuff that won't dissolve (like the skull, for instance), then you take out the meat and chop it up while the liquid reduces way down, thus concentrating the gelatin. Then you put it all together in loaf pans, or Jell-O molds, or what have you, and let it cool to set. I guess I could have said that head cheese is little more than a savory Jell-O mold, but I don't think you would have believed me.

41

couldn't do all the work themselves. So a kind of monetary system evolved in which the workers were paid in cardboard tokens (postwar monetary systems made cash a difficult proposition), which they could cash in at plantation "stores." Joan shows me a stack of such tokens along with a ledger showing the prewar value of all the slaves, which ranged from under ten to as high as fifteen hundred dollars.

The most fascinating part of the tour for me is the kitchen, kept in a separate building, as on most plantations, for the sake of isolating any accidental fire. There is an iron stove, a work table, and various countertop gadgets like apple corers and butter churns. I can't imagine making a peanut butter sandwich in this place, much less grand French cuisine, but in looking over the house receipts of the period, I find that that is indeed what was prepared. Dozens—maybe hundreds—of procedures, all handwritten in French, bear witness to the fact that, rough as life may have been, meal standards were maintained. I thank Joan and the Boudreaux family for sharing some of these precious family documents with us.

Sugar cane was the big crop at St. Joseph's, and the foundations of the old sugar mill still stand about half a mile behind the house. Since the fields are criss-crossed with excellent dirt roads, we decide to give our GSs the dirt baths they so richly deserve and go out to have a look. When we come back to the house an hour later we're greeted by a surreal sight. Two tour buses from Ole Miss have dumped a large load of hoopskirt-clad coeds and their string-tie tux–wearing beaus for a night of drunken revelry. Feeling and looking very out of place in our dirty duds, we depart with due haste.

BELOW LEFT: The front porch of St. Joseph's—originally huge canvas curtains were used to block the sun.
BELOW RIGHT: Extras from a *Gone With The Wind* remake? No, partyers from Ole Miss.
OPPOSITE: In the old kitchen at St Joseph's.

I'm not sure why they call this "bounce," but I can tell you it puts a bounce in your step. More than a few swigs and you're likely to find yourself in trouble.

CREOLE PLANTATION CHERRY BOUNCE

COURTESY OF ST. JOSEPH'S PLANTATION
VACHERIE, LOUISIANA

◆ ◆

> 1 pound Louisiana wild cherries or Bing cherries, washed and stemmed
> 14 ounces grain alcohol
> 2 cups granulated sugar
> 1 cup water

Put the cherries in a quart bottle and cover with enough grain alcohol to fill the bottle. Cork and let sit at room temperature for 6 to 8 weeks. Carefully strain the mixture through a fine-mesh sieve into a clean quart bottle, being sure to not mash the cherry pits.

In a 2-quart saucepan, bring the sugar and water to a boil over medium heat. Boil for 2 minutes, then remove from the heat. Let cool completely and store the sugar syrup in the refrigerator for up to 1 month.

Serve cherry liqueur over ice, with sugar syrup to taste.

YIELD: 14 OUNCES CHERRY LIQUEUR

OPPOSITE TOP: St. Joesph's Plantation— the openings along the ground floor were designed to channel flood waters.
OPPOSITE BOTTOM: Slave quarters.

Feed the poor and get rich or feed the rich and get poor.
COLONEL HARLAN SANDERS

The pecan

The pecan is the nut of the South and it finds its way into just about everything. I'd never thought of putting them in macaroons, though, because I suspected the fat from the nuts would deflate the foam. Luckily, it does not. If I were you, I'd take the time to toast the pecans before you chop them.

PECAN MACAROONS
COURTESY OF ST. JOSEPH'S PLANTATION
VACHERIE, LOUISIANA

✦ ✦

> 3 large egg whites
> 14 ounces granulated sugar
> 12½ ounces pecans, finely ground
> 1 teaspoon vanilla extract

Preheat the oven to 350 degrees.

Place the egg whites in the bowl of a stand mixer with the whisk attachment. Whisk on low speed for 2 to 3 minutes, until the egg whites begin to foam. Gradually add the sugar over 2 minutes. Increase the speed to high and whisk for another 10 minutes. This seems like a really long time, but it's not. Fold in the pecans and vanilla. Using a 2-tablespoon-size ice cream scoop, scoop the mixture onto parchment-lined half sheet pans. Bake for 14 to 17 minutes for a chewy macaroon and 17 to 20 minutes for a crisp macaroon. Rotate the pans 180 degrees halfway through the baking. The macaroons should be just brown around the edges. Remove the pan from the oven and place directly on a wet towel set on a heatproof surface. Let the cookies cool completely before removing from the pan.

YIELD: ABOUT 60 MACAROONS

ABOVE: On the road north of Laplace, Louisiana. The levee rises to the right, blocking our view of the river. We would sometimes ride all day without seeing it.

Although I wouldn't actually call this Southern classic "road food,"

this application from St. Joseph's Plantation is the best example of rice pudding I've ever tasted so I couldn't very well leave it out here.

RIZ AU LAIT

COURTESY OF ST. JOSEPH'S PLANTATION
VACHERIE, LOUISIANA

✦ ✦

½ cup uncooked white rice
1 quart whole milk
2 cups water
1 cup sugar
4 large egg yolks
½ teaspoon kosher salt
1 teaspoon vanilla extract
1 teaspoon cinnamon

In a 4-quart saucepan, combine the rice, milk, and water. Place over medium heat, cover, and bring to a simmer. Lower the heat and simmer for 45 minutes, stirring occasionally. Keep an eye on this, as the milk has a tendency to boil over. The rice should be fully cooked and soft. Remove from the heat.

When the rice is done, place the sugar and egg yolks in a medium mixing bowl and whisk to combine. Slowly add small amounts of the rice mixture to the egg mixture, whisking constantly. Once you have added half of the rice mixture to the egg and sugar, return this to the saucepan and place over low heat. Add the salt and vanilla and cook for 2 minutes, whisking constantly. Remove from the heat and ladle the pudding into 8 (8-ounce) ramekins. Sprinkle the top of each with a little cinnamon.

YIELD: 8 SERVINGS

NOTEBOOK ENTRY

The Great River Road was established in 1938 and is composed of a collection of federal, state, and local roads that coordinate through the Mississippi River Parkway Commission. The parkway sticks as close to the course of the river as possible through the ten states that border it: Louisiana, Mississippi, Arkansas (partial road only), Tennessee, Kentucky.

As far as I'm concerned, the evaporated milk makes this fudge by lending an ever-so-slightly burned flavor that I like very much. Pass the milk, if you please.

FUDGE À LA PAULINE
COURTESY OF ST. JOSEPH'S PLANTATION
VACHERIE, LOUISIANA

✦ ✦

> **21 ounces sugar**
> **1 tablespoon unsweetened cocoa powder**
> **1 (12-ounce) can evaporated milk**
> **4 ounces (1 stick) unsalted butter, plus more for the pan**
> **½ cup light corn syrup**
> **1 teaspoon vanilla extract**
> **Pinch of kosher salt**
> **4 ounces chopped pecans**

Butter an 8-inch-square metal pan.

In a 4-quart saucepan, whisk together the sugar and cocoa powder until well combined, with no lumps of cocoa. Add the evaporated milk, butter, and corn syrup. Place over medium heat and bring to 232 degrees, scraping down the sides of the pan and stirring occasionally with a wooden spoon. This should take 30 to 35 minutes.

Remove from the heat and add the vanilla, salt, and pecans. Beat with the wooden spoon until the mixture is spreadable and is no longer shiny, 7 to 8 minutes. Spread the fudge into the prepared pan and let the fudge cool completely at room temperature until set. Cut into 1-inch pieces and store in an airtight container for up to 1 week.

YIELD: 64 (1-INCH) PIECES

missouri, Illinois, Iowa, Wisconsin, and minnesota. Since it touches all these states it runs up both banks, which means you can go all the way up one side and down the other without repeating road. Although follow-ing it through cities is tough, the road is well marked with signs featuring a green pilot's wheel with a

riverboat in the mid-dle. They're small but easy to see. As might be expected, the views of the river are rather restricted in the south, where tall levees are the rule. Along the middle and upper river the views of the river, especial-ly from the bluffs, are astounding.

DAY FOUR

LIONEL KEY'S RESIDENCE
BATON ROUGE, LOUISIANA
0915 HOURS

Even through my helmet
I hear the beat as soon as I turn onto Beverly Drive. It's only mid-morning on a Sunday, but Lionel Key is already at it. We pull into the drive of a nice neat clapboard.

Out back, Lionel Key reaches into a burlap bag of dried sassafras leaves and deposits them into the hollowed center of a hunk of cypress stump. The device is as ancient as the matching four-foot pestle, which was passed down to Lionel by his great-uncle, who taught his nephew his craft. That is how to pound filé powder (aka gumbo filé), the mystical spice (okay, technically an herb) used to thicken soups and stews like gumbo.

NOTEBOOK ENTRY

Gumbo Filé: Many a hard-core Cajun cook has told me that gumbo should be thickened either with okra (the gooey mucilage inside does the trick) or filé, but never both. If you go with the filé, it can be added near the end of cooking and then again at the table. The roots of the sassafras tree were originally used to flavor root beer, but the leaves have a distinctive flavor all their own.

NOWHERE AS EASY
AS IT LOOKS.

Lionel starts out with the smooth, heavy pecan end of the stick, then switches to the rougher cypress end for grinding the shards of sassafras into a fine powder. The powder is then run through a sieve and a tamis (a very fine, drum-shaped sieve) to get all the stems out.

The powder coming out of Lionel's stump is not tan like the stuff from the grocery store or even olive drab like the cured leaves themselves. It's vivid green, almost chartreuse. He won't tell me where he picks the leaves or how he cures them. The one bone he throws me is that they often grow at fence lines where birds poop the seeds out. I pay him the fifteen bucks he's asking for a bottle that holds about two tablespoons of the powder. It's a good thing Lionel's got going here. When he asks where we're going next I say "north." He shakes his head and says, "Once you get outta Louisiana all the food is…" He makes a big, wet raspberry sound and that's all he needs to say. We thumb our starters, which almost drown out the sound of Lionel's beat, which, by the way, he swears the neighbors have gotten used to.

If you want to lay into some of Lionel Key's righteous powder, check out the list of sources on page 202.

ABOVE: Lionel's garden shrine.

NOTEBOOK ENTRY

In 1755 the British took possession of Acadia, an area composed of present-day Nova Scotia and Prince Edward Island, from France. The settlers there were given a choice: pledge allegiance to the British crown, or clear out. Many Acadians went back to France, or to prison, while many more headed south to Louisiana. It was a long, tortuous trip,

and those who survived did so in large part because of their ability to learn from the various Indian tribes they met along the way.

The Choctaw and Chickesaw peoples had been using various parts of the sassafras tree for centuries. A member of the laurel family, its bark and roots were brewed into medicinal tisanes and the leaves were ground

for soups and stews. Being French, the Acadians quickly recognized the powder's culinary value. Once they settled in Louisiana, the Acadians became known as cajun, and the rest is history.

I do not know why Camellia-brand red beans make the best rice and beans.

I used to think it was just a case of regional pride and preference, but having tested several other brands I have to agree that these beans are the best: creamy and flavorful. If I ever figure out the secret, I'll let you know.

RED BEANS, RICE, AND FILE

COURTESY OF LIONEL KEY'S HOUSE
BATON ROUGE, LOUISIANA

✦ ✦

1 pound Camellia red kidney beans*
1 quart water, plus extra for soaking
1 large yellow onion, chopped
3 tablespoons garlic powder
1 tablespoon freshly ground black pepper
1 tablespoon filé powder**
1 tablespoon kosher salt
3 to 4 cups hot cooked white rice

Cover the beans with water and soak overnight.

Drain the beans and discard the soaking water. In a 3½- to 4-quart saucepan, combine the beans, onion, garlic powder, pepper, filé, and salt. Add the water. If this does not completely cover the beans, add enough to do so. Cover and place over medium heat. Bring to a simmer, then lower the heat to maintain a simmer. Cook, stirring every 15 to 30 minutes, for 1½ hours. Reduce the heat to low and continue to cook for another 30 minutes. The beans should be tender and beginning to fall apart. Serve over rice.

YIELD: 8 TO 10 SERVINGS

*See the list of sources on page 202 to purchase.
**The quality of the filé is critical to the dish. I suggest you obtain a bottle from Lionel Key via his website. See the list of sources on page 202.

BELOW: Sassafras leaves come in three distinct shapes, but this mitten shape is the easiest to identify.
BOTTOM: Lionel Key explains the finer points of filé pounding.

We don't go anywhere. Going somewhere is for squares. We just go!
MARLON BRANDO, THE WILD ONE

✦ ✦ ✦ ✦ ✦ ✦ ✦ ✦ ✦

THE DONUT SHOP, NATCHEZ, MISSISSIPPI
1605 HOURS

Okay, I'm probably not supposed to eat donuts in the middle of the afternoon, but when I pass the Donut Shop on the edge of Natchez I can't help but yield to the yeasty siren song. The shop is built into an old gas station, and all of the donuts are lined up in the giant windows that probably used to house spare tires and pyramids of oil cans. And right in the middle there's a drive-through. Now, I'll admit there are other drive-through donut shops out there, but I've never seen one where you can actually see everything there is to choose from. Resistance is futile.

Shellie Wyant is working the window while Sheila Staples handles the glazing chores on the latest batch. I ask Shellie to pick one out for me, and she hands me a hot, yeasty, glazed number that looks plain but tastes ridiculously good. The glaze isn't quite set, so it gets all over my fingers—and my jacket, and the bike. I don't care. I order a dozen, though I have no idea where I'm going to carry them. Shellie loads up an assortment, including the best apple fritter I've ever had in my life. I don't care what else you do in Natchez, if you don't stop at the Donut Shop on John R. Junkin Drive, you're missing out.

BELOW: If you're headed into Natchez going north, this sight will be on your right. Don't fight the urge.

The word "fritter" is a corruption of *friture*, the French word for "fry." Come to think of it, everything about these fritters smacks of corruption. Corrupted morals, corrupted diets, corrupted willpower.

APPLE FRITTERS

INSPIRED BY A RECIPE FROM THE DONUT SHOP
NATCHEZ, MISSISSIPPI

✦ ✦

For the dough:

    1½ cups whole milk

    2½ ounces vegetable shortening (about ⅓ cup)

    2 (¼-ounce) packages active-dry yeast (2 scant tablespoons)

    ⅓ cup warm water (95 to 105 degrees)

    2 large eggs, beaten

    ¼ cup granulated sugar, plus 2 tablespoons for the filling

    1½ teaspoons kosher salt

    1 teaspoon freshly grated nutmeg

    23 ounces all-purpose flour, plus more for dusting the work surface

    1 pound finely chopped apples

    1 tablespoon freshly squeezed lemon juice

    3 tablespoons cinnamon

    Peanut or vegetable oil, for frying (1 to 1½ gallons, depending on the fryer), plus more for the bowl

For the fritter glaze:

    ½ cup plus 2 tablespoons whole milk

    1½ pounds confectioners' sugar

    1 teaspoon vanilla extract

Make the dough: Place the milk in a heatproof container and cook in a microwave oven for 1½ minutes. Carefully add the shortening to the milk and set aside. Make sure the shortening melts completely and that the mixture cools to lukewarm before adding to the other ingredients.

Continued on next page

BELOW: The donut sirens of Natchez. Tie yourself to the mast lest you gain three pounds on apple fritters.

Add the yeast, water, eggs, the ¼ cup sugar, the salt, the nutmeg, the milk and shortening mixture, and half of the flour to the bowl of a stand mixer. Using the paddle

attachment, combine the ingredients on low speed until the flour is incorporated, then turn the speed up to medium and beat until well combined. Add the remaining flour, combine on low speed at first, then increase the speed to medium and beat well. Change to the dough hook attachment and beat on medium speed until the dough pulls away from the bowl and becomes smooth, 3 to 4 minutes. Transfer to a well-oiled bowl, cover, and let rise for 1 hour or until doubled in size.

While the dough is rising, mix together the apples, lemon juice, the 2 tablespoons sugar, and the cinnamon in a medium bowl. Set aside.

On a well-floured work surface, roll the dough out to a 24-inch square. Evenly spread the apple mixture on the surface of the dough. Gently press the mixture into the dough. Starting at the bottom edge of the dough, roll into a log. Cut the log into 12 even pieces and lay each piece cut sides up and down. Cover with a tea towel and let rise for 30 minutes.

Make the fritter glaze: While the dough is rising for the last 30 minutes, whisk together the milk, confectioners' sugar, and vanilla in a medium saucepan over low heat. Remove the pan from the heat and set over a bowl of warm water in order to keep warm while frying the fritters.

Finish the fritters: In a deep fryer or Dutch oven, heat the oil to 350 degrees. Gently place the fritters in the oil, two at a time, and cook for 45 seconds per side. Transfer to a cooling rack placed in baking pan. Let cool just until able to handle. Dip the fritters into the glaze, one at a time, and return them to the cooling rack for 5 minutes before serving.

YIELD: 12 FRITTERS

✦ ✦ ✦ ✦ ✦ ✦ ✦ ✦ ✦

CLUB 601, NATCHEZ, MISSISSIPPI
1745 HOURS

Despite the fact that I was prepared to make camp back at the Donut Shop (there is, after all, the drive-through roof to keep me dry and plenty of deep-fried glazed goodness to keep me fat and happy), we've actually come to town in an effort to check out the blues festival that seems to be under way at locations all across town. We're told that Club 601 is doing fried catfish and spaghetti, and that is something I simply must try. We arrive at the pleasantly seedy club, which looks as though it's never been open during daylight hours, just before dinner. A joyous woman named Geraldine is getting ready to fry river cat, which she soaks in nothing but a little hot sauce before breading in cornmeal and dunking in hot oil. While waiting for the fish, I ask to sample the spaghetti, which tastes like nothing I've ever had. Actually that's not true. There is something about it that reminds me of the spaghetti they used to serve at my elementary school—but in a good way. The fact that it's being held in a huge dish on a warming tray only enhances this sensation. There is garlic, tomato of course, and several things I can't quite put my finger on, which drives me

BELOW: **Ramon the cameraman and Geraldine with their baby, a foil pan of freshly fried catfish, outside club 601, Natchez.**
OPPOSITE: **A good start at the Donut Shop.**

crazy. After I've pushed and prodded the effervescent Geraldine and her cooking partner, George Lee, for a good hour, they will admit only that it has zucchini in it, which I cannot imagine to be true. As they start serving plates I comment on the strange combination of fried fish and spaghetti but am quickly informed that this is a ubiquitous dish in these parts. As I scratch my head in an attempt to figure out what cultural or culinary forces could bring these things together, Bear leans over to me and whispers, "It's cheap."

Although I'm well versed in what the French call *cuisine de bonne femme*, I'd never thought for a moment that on this trip through the American heartland I would actually come face to face with dishes born of and sustained by poverty, despite the fact that evidence of deep impoverishment is all around me. Already on this trip we've seen neighborhoods of houses that I know didn't cost as much as my bike. You don't see this kind of thing from freeways—and you should.

NOTEBOOK ENTRY

Just for the record, river cat can be any species of catfish caught directly from the river (as opposed to a farmed variety). The most common cats (often referred to by anglers as mr. whiskers) are channel cats, flathead cats, white cats, and blue cats (which can get darned big, in excess of 120

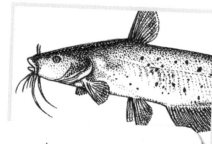

pounds). Although it's impossible to know what species you're eating once the beast is filleted, I'd bet that most of what we had on the trip was channel cat.

◆ ◆ ◆ ◆ ◆ ◆ ◆ ◆ ◆ ◆

DAY FIVE
NATCHEZ STATE PARK, MISSISSIPPI
0615 HOURS

If our first Feasting foray taught me anything, it's that you'd better be able to edit video as you go or you're doomed later on down the line. That requires a portable editing facility of some type, and since we also really needed some kind of mobile storage vessel and office, we have brought with us a thirty-six-foot Jayco motor home. It is called the Brown Flame, well, because it is brown and has flames on it. Bear takes care of and pilots the Flame, which is good because I don't even know how to turn it on.

BELOW: Hanging outside the Brown Flame in Natchez State Park.

On the evening of Day 4 we decide to bed down in Natchez State Park, which is a nice enough place. In the morning I decide to break in the Flame's galley.

Cooking in an RV is always an adventure, but when I discover that there's no salt on board my breakfast plan threatens to unravel. Egads, I already have the grits going, and no salt? I dispatch a scout to scour the park for sel and settle down to consider my options, which come down to: A. adapt to the situation, or B. panic. And I've never had a taste for panic.

Besides, Mr. Bailey back in Laplace threw us a lifeline by supplying us with both head cheese and andouille sausage—both fine sources of salt. I slice the sausage and brown it to render the fat. Meanwhile, I dice a jalapeño, part of an onion, and a small green pepper and add them to the pan. Next I have to deal with the lifeless and lackluster corn mush I've concocted. Head cheese contains mucho gelatin rendered from the porcine critter, and that will readily melt into the grits, suffusing the entire pot with an otherworldly goodness, not to mention plenty of salt. When the onions and peppers are soft, I throw in a dozen eggs and scramble them. Thanks to artisanal pork products, we have sustenance enough to face another day of...eating, mostly.

✦ ✦ ✦ ✦ ✦ ✦ ✦ ✦ ✦

OLD COUNTRY STORE, HIGHWAY 61, LORMAN, MISSISSIPPI
1320 HOURS

About an hour north of Natchez on Highway 61 is an old wooden building—over a hundred years old, in fact. Back in the 1920s it served as a social and mercantile center for the surrounding counties whose citizens came here to sell cotton, trade gossip, and buy everything from tobacco to shoes. Today it's part of the town of Lorman, though for the life of me I can't find any evidence of a town here. But people still come to Lorman from far and wide, because the current occupant of that building, the Old Country Store, is Arthur Davis, and what Arthur Davis does in the Old Country Store, and does better than any other living person, near as I can tell, is fry chicken. That's not actually fair: Arthur Davis cooks a lot of things but his chicken so overshadows everything else that it's tough to remember much else.

My own indoctrination to Davis chicken is a long time coming. Nearly an hour, I would say, because when we get here the whole crew is hungry. So I grab a camera and

OPPOSITE: **Bob, keeping in touch via Wireless Web.**
BELOW: **The Old Country Store in Lorman has been standing on this spot for over 100 years. It used to be the center of commerce for two counties.**

shoot. By the time I belly up to the buffet the chicken has, indeed, crossed the road. I watch everyone else eat while I shoot away with my handicam in a valiant attempt to make someone feel guilty enough to give me a piece of damn chicken. Fat chance.

I settle for some blackberry cobbler, which is good, though I'm suspicious as to where Davis would get said berries in April. Then just before I forlornly mount Buttercup, out bounds Davis with a huge plate of chicken. When he reaches me I kiss him soundly on his big, black cheek and tell him that I love him. He howls with laughter, then breaks into song (something he'll do if you hang around for more than three or four minutes). He likes to sing songs he's made up about his

grandmother, who he swears is frying chicken in heaven. I take the first bite of what seems like the first chicken I've ever eaten. A perfectly crunchy exterior cloaks moist, flavorful

meat that actually tastes like chicken. It's so hot I can barely chew it, but I manage. As soon as I swallow, I turn on him. "This isn't grocery-store chicken! Who's your supplier?" He won't tell me, of course, though he mentions several times that it's "fresh, fresh, fresh." I ask if he's killing them out back, and he only says that they're not quite that fresh. I ask him about his breading, and again...nothing. He uses flour and something he calls "shake," which is of course a secret. I push him for facts and he sings again and eventually, after I've downed another thigh and a breast (historically my least favorite piece of bird), I join him in an impromptu blues duet about a mean man who won't give the chicken secrets away.

I'm grateful that Arthur Davis exists and that there are enough people in the land who care about his craft to drive great distances to reach him. If you're in Lorman, or within ten states of Lorman, consider making the trip.

✦ ✦ ✦ ✦ ✦ ✦ ✦ ✦ ✦ ✦

BIEDENHARN CANDY CO. AND COCA-COLA MUSEUM, VICKSBURG, MISSISSIPPI
1600 HOURS

BELOW: An American classic rolls through Vicksburg.
OPPOSITE: Bieden- harn Candy Co. has been on Washington Street for over a hundred years.

I've come here to visit the Biedenharn Candy Co. and Coca-Cola Museum. Joseph Biedenharn is one of the great heroes of American cuisine and a real-life Willy Wonka. The museum houses a replica of Biedenharn's bottling lab, which is a sight no food geek should miss.

Biedenharn's museum also includes a large and unique collection of Coca-Cola arti- facts and memorabilia reflecting the evolution not only of a product but of the culture that elevated it. If you're in Vicksburg, don't miss it.

In 1862, Herman Biedenharn started making candy in Vicksburg, Mississippi. His son, Joe, was born in 1866 and was raised in the business, becoming an expert in every facet of confectionery. He was especially interested in soda. Back then, confectioners made their own carbonated water via a complex and rather dangerous system that captured the CO_2 from marble chips dissolved in hydrochloric acid. This "soda" was then mixed with a fla- vored syrup by a soda jerk. (The "jerk" moniker came from the motion required to turn the carbonic flow on and off.) Hoping to provide products like fizzy lemonade to folks in the

surrounding countryside who didn't get into town very often, Joe Biedenharn undertook the development of a system that would bottle sodas one pressurized, rubber-stopped vessel at a time. While this was going on, a salesman came into town from Atlanta offering a new kind of soda syrup that was going to be a big hit. It was called Coca-Cola. The bever- age sold remarkably well at the shop, and it wasn't long before Biedenharn decided it was time to put Coca-Cola in a bottle. This seems a quaint notion now, but back then no one had seen it coming. Sodas like Coca-Cola were assembled and served at soda fountains (Coca-Cola creator John Pemberton was, after all, a pharmacist). The fountain itself was a social center and remained one through my own mother's youth. In my opinion, Biedenharn unleashed the modern age, in which a nation could be galvanized by a beverage that would then go on to be one of the first planetary corporations. Is this any less a development than those of Bell, Edison, Marconi, Tesla? I think not.

ABOVE: Biedenharn's got the best collection of Coke memorabilia outside Atlanta.
RIGHT: Soda taps.
OPPOSITE: Recreating history: actors reenact the making of soda water. Dangerous business...
OPPOSITE BOTTOM: The battle of Vicksburg.

In 1860 Vicksburg was a sleepy little town with no war-related industry and no real rail center. But it stood (and stands) on a tall bluff overlooking a hairpin turn in the river. When war broke out, Confederate forces placed large cannons on the bluff and in doing so took control of all traffic moving up and down the river.

Lincoln knew that without the key of Vicksburg in his pocket the war would not be won. So he sent his favorite pit bull, Ulysses S. Grant, to take care of the situation. Vicksburg eventually fell, but only after several failed attacks and a long, bloody siege that lasted through the spring and summer of 1863.

69

SOUL FOOD SURVIVOR

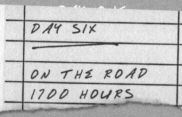

DAY SIX

ON THE ROAD
1700 HOURS

Stretching from Vicksburg to Memphis is a jet-black eye of alluvial plain five thousand square miles flat, cradled by the Mississippi on one side and the Yazoo on the other. This is the Delta that David L. Cohn described best in his 1948 memoir, *Where I Was Born and Raised*. He called the Delta "a strange and detached fragment thrown off by the whirling comet that is America."

Cotton is still king here, but the Delta's most cherished crop is the blues, arguably the only true American musical form and the undisputed father of rock and roll (gospel being the mother, I suppose). All the greats are from the Delta: B. B. King, Muddy Waters, and of course Robert Johnson, who supposedly traded his soul to the Devil in exchange for musical powers at a lonely intersection in Clarksdale, Mississippi. Lucky for us, the Delta is also culinarily fertile. Especially when it comes to tamales.

✦ ✦ ✦ ✦ ✦ ✦ ✦ ✦ ✦ ✦

JIM'S CAFE, GREENVILLE, MISSISSIPPI
0912 HOURS

Downtown Greenville is all but a ghost town. Countless businesses have closed along Washington Avenue, despite the opening of a casino within sight, on the river. There's one eatery open: Jim's Café. We need breakfast. We go in. The walls of Jim's are lined with ancient photos, most of them cleverly labeled with Dynotape. Remember Dynotape? There are familiar faces here, a signed photo of Faulkner and one of Jacques-Yves Cousteau from when the Calypso got stuck in the river. There are stuffed fish and birds, too, and various riverboat knickknacks. The walls are dark panelling. Everything is dark except through the kitchen door comes a brilliant slash of yellow and green. I push toward it and encounter a crisp but not exactly friendly waitress named Barbara Coveney, who lets us know right away that there is no way she's appearing on television. I try to comfort her with the knowledge that I would not dream of letting her ever be on television but this doesn't really help. After explaining our mission, I request permission to see the kitchen but am told

BELOW RIGHT:
Shooting in the kitchen at Jim's Café, Greenville, Mississippi.

that the owner wouldn't like it. I ask her with a wink if she's ever done anything the owner didn't like. This gets me a giggle and access is suddenly no longer denied.

✦ ✦ ✦ ✦ ✦ ✦ ✦ ✦ ✦

The cook is Ms. Clara Brantely, and it's clear she's a career cook. She would never call herself a chef; she says they just mess things up. It's the end of breakfast service, so we'd better order fast. I'm thinking pancakes when I smell pork. Turns out about an hour ago, Ms. Brantely parboiled some pork rib tips in seasoned broth and then moved them to the oven to bake long and low with her barbecue sauce, which she unabashedly admits came from "that jug over there." She cracks the oven door for me and lets me probe the tasty mass with a clean finger. I taste it. Sweet. The sauce even has traces of maple in it. Maple... pancakes...maple...barbecue...rib tips...pancakes.

Within fifteen minutes we're all eating barbecued pork rib tips on cornmeal pancakes. I would tell you they're good—beyond good. But unless you're in driving range of Jim's Café in Greenville, Mississippi, I figure it would be kinda mean to rub your nose in it.

If I'm ever put in a position where I am able to choose my last breakfast on earth, I pick this barbecue served atop cornmeal pancakes. Hold the syrup.

BBQ PORK RIBS, AKA "BREAKFAST RIBS"

COURTESY OF JIM'S CAFÉ
GREENVILLE, MISSISSIPPI

+ +

> 2 onions, chopped
> 2 cloves garlic, chopped
> 2 stalks celery, chopped
> 4 pounds country-style pork ribs
> 1 tablespoon kosher salt
> 2 teaspoons freshly ground black pepper
> 3 tablespoons beef base
> 1 (28-ounce) bottle of your
>   favorite barbecue sauce
> 2 teaspoons hot sauce

OPPOSITE: **Clara Brantely, head cook at Jim's Café, has been cooking for most of her sixty-eight years.**
BELOW: **Coming soon to a fashionable eatery near you: barbecue on pancakes.**

Preheat the oven to 350 degrees.

Fill a 10-quart stockpot half full of water. Add the onions, garlic, and celery and bring to a boil over high heat. While the water is coming to a boil, toss the ribs with the salt and pepper. Once the water comes to a boil, add the beef base and the ribs. Parboil the ribs for 40 minutes.

Remove the ribs from the stockpot and place them in a large roasting pan. Pour 1 cup of the cooking water into the roasting pan. Roast for 45 minutes, or until tender. Remove from the oven.

Combine the barbecue sauce with the hot sauce and spread over the ribs, tossing to coat well. Return to the oven for 15 minutes, or until warmed through.

YIELD: 4 TO 6 SERVINGS

✦ ✦ ✦ ✦ ✦ ✦ ✦ ✦ ✦

DOE'S EAT PLACE, NELSON ST., GREENVILLE, MISSISSIPPI
1047 HOURS

Doe's Eat Place isn't just a Greenville institution, it's an American institution, one that's been honored with fans from around the world and a James Beard American Classics award, which isn't exactly an easy thing to finagle. Doe's has been run by the Signa family since it was a grocery store back in the 1940s. It eventually evolved into a Honky Tonk and then a restaurant. Besides ridiculously thick broiled steaks (I can testify as to the quality of the porterhouse) and one of the best tossed salads I've ever consumed, there are tamales made with an ancient tamale machine that looks like something Henry Ford would have concocted. Three generations of the Signa family now work the place and the current matriarch, Barbara Signa, shows me the side dining room and explains how it used to be the kid's bedroom. Trust me, this family is invested in this place, which looks like...well, shack chic is the only way I can think to put it. Both of the main rooms are part kitchen and cooking happens right next to tables, something that would never be allowed in this day of safety regulations. Lucky for Doe's, their current configuration was grandfathered in.

After trying my hand at tamale rolling (pathetic), we sit down to a feast, the likes of which we will never see again on this journey. And I have to say, it's the best steak I've ever had in my life. Broiling is part of the secret, but there's something else they're not telling me... And since this is the South, secrets are serious business. In fact, Barbara tells me that before Little Doe married her way back when, his father warned him against sharing the family's secret tamale recipe with an outsider. To this day she swears she doesn't know it. When I imply that this is perhaps unfair, she says it's not a problem because she's the one who knows where the money is. And so another one of life's little equations balances out. Full and grateful, we ride on.

BELOW: Porterhouse in all its glory.
OPPOSITE: Cale Caruthers and Earnest Hardy take a break.

✦ ✦ ✦ ✦ ✦ ✦ ✦ ✦ ✦

JOE'S WHITE FRONT CAFE, ROSEDALE, MISSISSIPPI
1347 HOURS

The Delta is a mysterious place in a heap of ways, but right now the disconcerting mystery I'm out to solve is strictly culinary: How did the hot tamale get here?

Everywhere you turn, someone's makin', sellin', or eatin' hot tamales. Not just tamales, mind you, but "hot" tamales. It's been this way since 1936, when the great (and certainly mysterious) bluesman Robert Johnson wrote his classic song *Hot Tamales*. In fact, it is said that Robert Johnson traded his soul to the devil in return for supernatural musical abilities one dark midnight at a crossroad outside of Clarksdale. Satan actually capped the deal by telling Johnson to go on into town and get himself a plate o' hot tamales. He said that Johnson would need somethin' in his belly where he was going.

Unlike Latin American tamales, Delta hot tamales are always simmered in a flavorful broth, never steamed. And this broth is extremely aromatic. At least it is out on Main Street in Rosedale. I look to the dilapidated facade of Joe's White Front Café and out comes Amy Evans, who I am hoping will set my twitchin' mind to ease on the subject. She's with the Southern Foodways Alliance, an excellent organization run out of Oxford, Mississippi. Amy's just finished a web-based documentary on what in these parts is called the "tamale trail," which runs up the river from Vicksburg to Memphis. Joe's White Front is one of her favorite stops on the trail.

Amy takes me in and introduces me to Barbara Pope, who moved down from Chicago a couple of years ago when her brother Joe got sick. He died in 2005, so now Barbara keeps the place going. Inside, the White Front is sparse, clean, and friendly. There's not much in the way of decoration: a couple of tables and a counter half covered with jars of old-fashioned candies and a gallon jug of what appears to be bright pink dill pickles. Having never seen a bright pink dill pickle, I make inquiries.

Amy: *They're Koolickles.*
Me: *Of course they are. Um...*
Amy: *Pickles soaked in Kool-Aid.*
Me: *Ms. Barbara, did you invent that?*
Barbara: *Lord, no. You can get them all over here.*
Me: *Ms. Barbara?*
Barbara: *Yes?*
Me: *Why?*
Barbara: *They taste good. Have one.*
Me: *(Gulp) Okay.*

Tongs emerge. Ms. Barbara reaches in and extracts one of the slimy, pink things. It looks more like a bloated tongue than a cucumber, and yet something about the jewel-

It is not down in any map; true places never are.
HERMAN MELVILLE

toned blimp is appealing. She puts the full-sized dill on a plate. My pocket knife is out in a flash, and I carve off a few hunks. The smell of pickles is heavy in the air. I bring it to my mouth, but flash back to other smelly pink things I've put in my mouth on the road. Like pickled pigs' feet (shiver). In it goes. I chew, and...well, it's a pickle for sure. Full-on sour, dill but not kosher, and tasting of cherry. Tart but sweet, fruity but fully committed to the briny character of the original. It's savory and sweet, reminding me of certain Japanese desserts I've had. Actually, this would go pretty well with sushi.

Me: *I must know who came up with this.*
Amy: *Nobody knows.*
Barbara: *(Shakes head) Nobody.*

Make up a jar and keep them on your counter or, better yet, in your fridge. I promise that unless you live in the Delta you'll be the first in your neighborhood to serve them. Strange though they are, these bright pink beauties are extraordinarily refreshing on a hot summer day.

KOOLICKLES

ROAD INSPIRED

1 gallon jar kosher dill pickles
2 packages unsweetened cherry Kool-Aid
1 pound sugar

Drain the liquid from the pickles into a large container. Add the Kool-Aid mix and the sugar to the liquid and stir until the sugar is completely dissolved. Remove the pickles from the jar, slice them in half lengthwise, and return them to the jar. Return the liquid to the jar of pickles. Not all of the liquid will fit, but make sure the pickles are completely covered. Place in the refrigerator and let sit for 1 week before eating.

YIELD: 1 GALLON KOOLICKLES

Yes, they take a little time and effort to make, but once you get the hang of it they come together very quickly. I suggest you teach a few of your friends how to form the tamales, then have yourself a tamale bee, where you make a zillion or so and divvy them up. I probably consumed a hundred tamales during my time in the Delta, but no one ever gave me even a slight hint as to what might be in that broth. You have to remember that down here the Devil is said to walk around like a man, so folks hold close what's dear.

MISSISSIPPI DELTA TAMALES
COURTESY OF TAMALETRAIL.COM

✦ ✦

For the meat filling:

    6 to 8 pounds boneless pork shoulder, chuck roast, or chicken

    ¾ cup vegetable oil

    ¼ cup chili powder

    2 tablespoons paprika

    2 tablespoons kosher salt

    1 tablespoon onion powder

    1 tablespoon garlic powder

    2 teaspoons black pepper

    1 teaspoon cayenne pepper

    1 teaspoon ground cumin

For the corn husks:

    7 to 8 dozen corn husks

For the cornmeal dough:

    8 cups yellow cornmeal or masa mix

    4 teaspoons baking powder

    2 teaspoons salt

    1⅔ cups lard or vegetable shortening

    6 to 8 cups of the broth from cooking the meat, warm

Continued on next page

BELOW: Although most of the tamales we consumed in Mississippi were wrapped in traditional corn husks, at Doe's they wrap them in parchment paper and bundle them in threes. If you scratch the picture you can actually smell the cumin.

Make the meat filling: Cut the meat into large chunks and place in a large, heavy pot. Cover with cold water. Bring to a boil over high heat. Cover the pot, reduce the heat to medium-low, and simmer until the meat is very tender, 2 to 2 ½ hours. Remove the meat and reserve the cooking liquid. When the meat is cool enough to handle, remove and discard any skin and large chunks of fat. Shred or dice the meat into small pieces. There should be 14 to 16 cups of meat. Heat the oil in a large, heavy pot over medium heat. Stir in the chili powder, paprika, salt, onion powder, garlic powder, black pepper, cayenne, and cumin. Add the meat and stir to coat with the oil and spices. Cook, stirring often, until the meat is warmed through, 7 to 10 minutes. Set aside.

Prepare the corn husks: While the meat is cooking, soak the husks in a large bowl or sink of very warm water until they are soft and pliable, about 2 hours. Gently separate the husks into single leaves, trying not to tear them. Wash off any dust and discard any corn silks. Keep any shucks that split to the side, since two small pieces can be overlapped and used as one.

Make the cornmeal dough: Stir the cornmeal, baking powder, salt, and lard together in a large bowl until well blended. Gradually stir in enough warm broth to make soft, spongy dough that is the consistency of thick mashed potatoes. The dough should be quite moist, but not wet. Cover the bowl with a damp cloth.

Assemble the tamales: Remove a corn husk from the water and pat it dry. Lay the husk on a work surface. Spread about ¼ cup of the dough in an even layer across the wide end of the husk to within 1 inch of the edges. Spoon about 1 tablespoon of the meat filling in a line down the center of the dough. Roll the husk so that the dough surrounds the filling and forms a cylinder or package. Fold the bottom under to close the end and complete the package. Place the completed tamales in a single layer on a baking sheet. Repeat until all the dough and filling are used.

Cook the tamales:
To simmer: Stand the tamales upright, closed side down, in a large pot. Place enough tamales in the pot so that they do not fall over or come unrolled. Carefully fill the pot with enough water to come just to the top of the tamales, trying not to pour water directly into the tamales. Bring the water to a boil over high heat. Cover the pot, reduce the heat to medium-low, and simmer until the dough is firm and pulls away from the husk easily and cleanly, about 1 hour.

To steam: Stand the tamales upright, closed side down, in a large steamer basket. Cover the tamales with a damp towel or additional husks. Steam the tamales over simmering water until the dough is firm and pulls away from the husk easily and cleanly, 1 to 1¼ hours.

Serve the tamales warm, in their husks. Remove the husks to eat.

YIELD: 7 TO 8 DOZEN TAMALES

✦ ✦ ✦ ✦ ✦ ✦ ✦ ✦ ✦

DAY SEVEN
RAY'S DAIRY MAID, BARTON, ARKANSAS
0825 HOURS

I'm standing outside Ray's Dairy Maid, on Highway 49 outside of Helena–West Helena, Arkansas. Like so many roadside joints, Ray's has a dining room and a walk-up window, probably left over from its dairy days. There hasn't been a Ray here in a long time, and the only maid is the present owner, a round pixie in her sixties named Deane Cavette, aka Nana Deane. When I first meet Nana Deane, she's making meringue pies, a bold move considering it's pouring rain. I think she's got enough sweetened, whipped egg white in her mixing bowl for three pies, but as she talks she just keeps piling it on one particular coconut cream, higher and higher—close to eight inches, I'd say. She slides the tower into an ancient oven and sets a timer (the first such device I've seen on this trip). She heads up into the main kitchen and starts firing western omelettes. Apparently she is the only cook here allowed to fire the famed western, and it's a deft performance. Clearly she's spent

BELOW: Sanctuary from heavy rains in Arkansas.

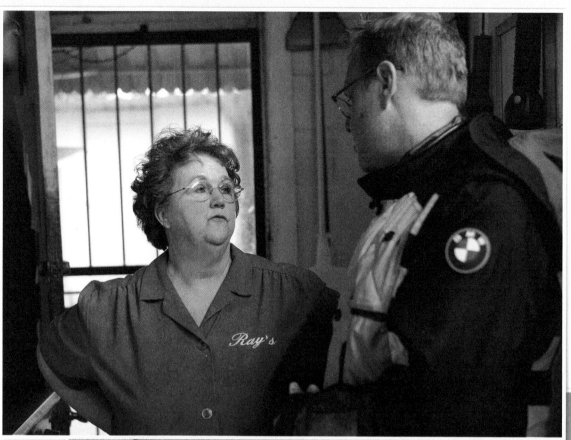

plenty of time at the flat-top (which folks around here insist on calling a grill). She starts the eggs on one side while sautéing the veggies on the other. The spatula never rests, and neither does Nana Deane's voice. She can talk a blue streak and tell a story, and she's a natural host. When she turns to the TV camera and just goes with it, I worry for my job. I start wondering if I could sign her to a contract, but I don't want to ruin the moment. A couple of flicks from the spat and it looks like an eggy python has consumed a vegetable patch. It's fat and round and completely neat. Then another trick. She takes three triangles of American cheese and, holding them by one tip, dips them into the fryolator before placing them on top of the python. In seconds, the cheesefood has melted into a silky (if not slightly gross) blanket. Deep-fat-fried fat. Just think of it.

She sends the omelette out to the dining room and turns to see two guys huddled by the order window. Tough-looking guys, but they smile at her. Nana Deane holds up a finger to let them know she knows. She looks around, finds a bag by the griddle, and takes it over to them. They're regulars and didn't have to order. It was waiting for them when they got there. When I ask the two petroleum workers (there's some kind of oil works nearby), they tell me Nana Deane is like their mom. One admits to being fed by her six days a week. When I ask him who feeds him on the seventh he smiles sheepishly and says, "My other momma."

The timer goes off but Nana Deane's busy with another one of her kids, so I go back and pull the pie out and know the moment I lay eyes on it that I am going to eat it...or at least most of it. I decide to sneak it through the kitchen to the dining room, but not before grabbing a pecan coconut pie off the shelf to keep it company.

In ten minutes there's nothing left but two tin pans and ten guys rubbing their stomachs. We all decide that the pecan coconut is our favorite and—lo and behold—Nana Deane graces us with the recipe. The rain stops, the clouds part, and there are no longer any acceptable excuses to tarry, which makes me a bit sad. Nana Deane and her kitchen girls ask for pictures with all of us and so do some of the customers. We happily oblige and ride on to Helena–West Helena.

OPPOSITE TOP: **Nana Deane giving a lesson in pie philosophy.** OPPOSITE BOTTOM: **"Scratch" biscuits at Ray's.** BELOW: **The queen in her castle.**

This is the pie coconut was created for.

NANA DEANE'S PECAN COCONUT PIE

COURTESY OF RAY'S DAIRY MAID
BARTON, ARKANSAS

+ +

OPPOSITE: Two coco-
nut pies, cream and
pecan-coconut. Some
of the best pies of
the trip.

10½ ounces sugar
3 large eggs
2 ounces (½ stick) unsalted butter, melted and cooled slightly
4 ounces buttermilk
3 ounces sweetened shredded coconut
3 ounces chopped pecans (about ¾ cup)
1 tablespoon all-purpose flour
1 teaspoon vanilla extract
Pinch of salt
Prebaked 9-inch pie crust

Preheat the oven to 350 degrees.

In a large mixing bowl, combine the sugar, eggs, butter, buttermilk, coconut, pecans, flour, vanilla, and salt. Pour into the pie crust. Bake for 45 minutes, or until the pie is golden brown and the center is barely set. Let cool for 40 to 45 minutes before serving.

YIELD: 1 (9-INCH) PIE

NOTEBOOK ENTRY

It is a wonder that anyone in the old south lives to see fifty. In the ten days that we've been on the road I have seen and consumed more fatty, starchy, and fried foods than in any period before in my life. It is amazing. These foods are cherished here above all others. Here is the problem: there's no balance. These folks eat like they did when the South was still a rural and agrarian society. They're just not burning the calories anymore. Of course there are some exceptions to the bad nutrition rule. In Louisiana we saw a lot of red beans and rice, which, if cooked properly, provides a complete protein with very little fat. But of course it's still starchy as all get-out. It is no wonder that people in the Delta have some of the worst health records in the united states. Of course, you're talkin' to a guy who just ate two pieces of pie for breakfast!

✦ ✦ ✦ ✦ ✦ ✦ ✦ ✦ ✦ ✦

DELTA CULTURAL CENTER, HELENA–WEST HELENA, ARKANSAS
1200 HOURS

Helena–West Helena, as the combined town is now called, is home to the Delta Cultural Center, headquarters of the legendary King Biscuit Time radio show, which is the longest-running show in all of radio and still broadcasts Monday through Friday at 12:15 p.m. on 1360 AM. Since the 1960s, King Biscuit Time has been hosted by Sunshine Sonny Payne, who has been credited with influencing generations of artists from Elvis to Clapton to the Stones. For some strange reason, Sunshine Sonny Payne wants me on the show. Maybe it's just a slow day in Helena–West Helena, but then even on slow days people like Robert Plant have just dropped by for a visit—so anything can happen. I sit at a mike and the show begins with Sonny's line "Pass the biscuits." But it doesn't take much talkin' for me to realize that ole Sunshine Sonny doesn't have a single clue as to who I am. He's darned nice to me anyway and keeps us talking about food in between songs. He goes on about how he makes eggplant Parmesan, a favorite of his, but when I ask him how often he makes it he says, "Once a year." Funny guy, that Sunshine Sonny Payne. He closes by telling all the housewives out there to get cookin'. Brave man, that Sunshine Sonny Payne.

TOP OPPOSITE: By the tracks in Helena–West Helena. BELOW: I've been a fan of Sonny's since childhood. He doesn't know me from Adam but, man, is he nice.

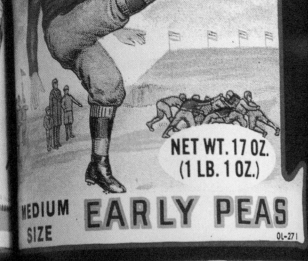

NET WT. 17 OZ.
(1 LB. 1 OZ.)

MEDIUM
SIZE
EARLY PEAS

OL-271

NET WT. 1
(1 LB. 1 O

MEDIUM
SIZE
EARLY P

SCHOOL DAYS

SD

MEDIUM
SIZE

SCHOOL DA

SD

DON'T LOOK FOR
SCHOOL DAYS ON YOUR
SHELVES. THE BRAND
WENT BELLY UP OVER
50 YEARS AGO.

NET W
(1 LB.

MEDIUM
SIZE
EARLY

.07

✦ ✦ ✦ ✦ ✦ ✦ ✦ ✦ ✦

DAY EIGHT
PINK PALACE MUSEUM, MEMPHIS, TENNESSEE
1600 HOURS

One of the few stops that we actually planned on this trip is the Pink Palace in Memphis, home to a reconstructed full-scale model of the first Piggly Wiggly grocery store. What, you might ask, does a grocery store have to do with road food? A lot, when you consider that the modern grocery store was made possible by the automobile.

Once upon a time, the general store was king. Every town had one and it carried everything that you couldn't make for yourself down on the farm. To order, you came in and gave your list to a clerk, who then filled the order while you waited or hung out in the saloon. In many cases a boy on a bicycle would deliver the order to your house. It was a good system. But then came the automobile. Armed with a Model A or T, country folk could get to town whenever they wanted. The influx of traffic and people stressed the general store system beyond its limits. That's when Clarence Saunders had a wacky and wonderful idea that changed the world forever: the supermarket.

On September 6, 1916, the first Piggly Wiggly market, on Jefferson Street in Memphis, Tennessee, opened its doors. The shopper began her odyssey by passing through a device called a turnstile (a Saunders invention). The shopper then grabbed an empty basket and moved down a winding series of narrow aisles, each side of which was stocked with individually priced items, many of which were nationally advertised brands. (This doesn't sound too innovative, but keep in mind that no one had done any of this before, not even the package pricing.) Although lilliputian by today's standards, in 1916 the tiny store was considered a consumer's cornucopia. There were even refrigerated cases for things like milk and butter, a fresh produce section, and a checkout stand where each item could be "rung up" on a cash register. Piggly Wiggly was such a success that by 1922 it had opened twelve hundred stores in twenty-nine states.

After losing control of his own creation in the mid-1920s, Saunders turned his attention to the development of a completely automated grocery store he called Keedoozle and then Foodelectric. You haven't heard of these. Few have. Saunders was just too far ahead of his time.

The Pink Palace, by the way, was built by Saunders to be his personal home. He lost it, along with most of what he owned, before his death in 1953.

OPPOSITE: **One of the coolest things about the Piggly Wiggly exhibit is the period products lining the shelves. Looking at this can, it's easy to see how the whole celebrity endorsement thing got started.**
BELOW: **In Memphis there's an impressive museum called the Pink Palace, built as the Xanadu of Clarence Saunders, the inventer of the modern grocery store. He died broke. The general store display inside the museum (which has a little bit of every-thing) includes this barrel, which, judg-ing from the smell, housed salt pork.**

✦ ✦ ✦ ✦ ✦ ✦ ✦ ✦ ✦ ✦

JIM NEELY'S INTERSTATE BAR-B-QUE, MEMPHIS, TENNESSEE
1820 HOURS

One thing is for sure: There is no restaurant in Memphis that doesn't serve some form of barbecue. I don't know if it's a city ordinance or a tradition or a simple response to the expectations of visitors to this fair city, but barbecue is indeed everywhere, and 95 percent of it is just plain bad. In fact, very few people actually know where to go for good Q in Memphis. Most aficionados claim three high churches of the craft: the famed Rendezvous, Corky's, and Jim Neely's Interstate Bar-B-Que. Neely's is a family operation through and through, and has been for twenty-eight years. The night we roll in Kelvin Neely, one of Jim Neely's sons, is at the rudder. We're unannounced, of course, but even though it's a Friday night he's willing to show us around the place. There are two kitchens at Neely's: the restaurant kitchen, which produces Q for the dining room, takeout, and the drive-through window, and a separate one for mail-order.

✦ ✦ ✦ ✦ ✦ ✦ ✦ ✦ ✦ ✦

Stacked in a bin in the back of the kitchen are huge sheets of cracklins. Cracklins are nothing more nor less than fried (or sometimes roasted) pig skins, and these are perfect: crunchy, porky, and salty. We visit the main barbecue oven, or "pit," so named because it's so black inside it looks like a pit. This pit is fed by wood smoke from outside. Currently some whole shoulders are roasting away under a thin layer of dry rub, which is all good

OPPOSITE: Kelvin Neely, before the pit.
BELOW: Pork cracklins at Interstate.

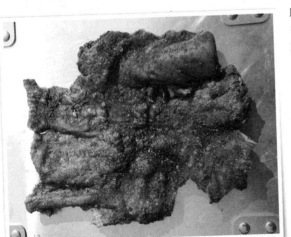

pork really needs. Then in a separate building there's a USDA food production facility where ribs and other products are prepped, packed, and frozen for shipping all around the country. What the Neelys have is a little barbecue empire. This bigness makes me immediately suspicious. In the world of food, rarely does one find industrial expansion coexisting with authenticity. My fears, however, are put to rest when the Q comes to the table. It is well cooked, properly smoked, and darned good. And it has strange plate buddies. There is, for instance, barbecued baloney and barbecued spaghetti. Although the baloney is too sweet for me, the spaghetti is really something. Somehow it doesn't seem out of place among barbecue and barbecue sauce. But my favorite thing at Neely's are the ribs. I'm picky about ribs. They must be cooked so that the meat gives up the bone but not without a little fight. That's exactly what Neely's back ribs do, and beautifully so. Although the hot sauce (which Kelvin tells me he makes ten pots of every night) is a well-balanced elixir, I have my ribs straight from the pit dressed only in time, heat, smoke, and Neely's dry rub.

What I like best about Neely's, however, is watching Kelvin's crew at work. The atmosphere is genial and upbeat. People cut up, play practical jokes. It's a nice place to hang out. Kelvin claims that the whole operation is what it is because his dad makes it that way. But I sense that the entire family holds this place near and dear. The extra distance they're willing to go has an effect on everyone in the place.

Every BBQ place on earth serves slaw. I like to put it right on my pulled pork sandwich so that I get some in every bite. This particular recipe is an amalgam of a dozen different versions we encountered. Use a box grater to get the texture just right, or use a knife. Avoid the food processor.

DELTA COLE SLAW
ROAD INSPIRED

✦ ✦

1¼ cups mayonnaise
2 tablespoons sweet pickle relish
1 tablespoon cider vinegar
1 teaspoon kosher salt
¼ teaspoon freshly ground black pepper
1 head green cabbage, grated
2 carrots, grated

In a large mixing bowl, whisk together the mayonnaise, relish, vinegar, salt, and pepper. Add the cabbage and carrots and toss to combine. Cover, place in the refrigerator, and let sit for at least 1 hour before serving.

YIELD: 6 TO 8 SERVINGS

We should look for someone to eat and drink with before looking for something to eat and drink.
EPICURUS

◆ ◆ ◆ ◆ ◆ ◆ ◆ ◆ ◆

DAY NINE
WILES–SMITH DRUGS, MEMPHIS, TENNESSEE
0949 HOURS

Deciding that motorcycles aren't the ideal vehicles for navigating an edible tour of Memphis, we rent a gigantic 1976 Cadillac Eldorado, which holds seven of us comfortably and three more in the trunk. We're not sure where we're headed, but somehow we end up on Union Avenue. That's where we see Wiles-Smith Drugs, its windows clearly lined with booths, and that means there's got to be either a lunch counter or a full-blown fountain. Turns out the pharmacy has been open for sixty years and is apparently the only pharmacy in the area with its original fountain intact and working. There's even a full—albeit small—kitchen. The cook is Miss Vaughn, and she's been at this quite a while. Her specialty is a chicken salad that she makes every day from fresh-cooked chicken. She uses both light and dark meat and she hand-grates the eggs and, yes, that makes a difference (lighter texture, don't ya know). A little mayonnaise, some pickle relish, a bit of salt and black pepper—it's delicious.

BELOW: A 1976 Eldorado—'nuff said.

But the real specialty of the house is a curious concoction called a Cherry Joe. A few years back, a guy named Joe worked the fountain counter and he liked making shakes that were very, very thick. So thick that you had to pry them out of the glass. Now, one of the pharmacists (don't know if it was Smith or Wiles) used to concoct a homemade cherry syrup that they put in kids' cough medicines. Well, one day Joe decided to use this syrup to make a shake, and thus was born the Cherry Joe. The Cherry Joe is a satisfying curiosity. It is a shake, to be sure, and darned if it doesn't taste like cough syrup—but as Mary Poppins would say, "in the most delightful way." I finish my chicken-salad sandwich and my entire Cherry Joe. Then I go outside and start my new postmeal regimen: twenty push-ups and twenty sit-ups. Miss Vaughn comes out to bid us a fond farewell, and since she seems to know her stuff we ask about lunch. I mention the fact that we haven't had much in the way of vegetables in the last few days, and so Miss Vaughn steers us to Melanie's Soul Food in north Memphis. We load up the Caddy and proceed with due haste. After all, it's lunchtime.

BELOW: **Linda Spencer whips up a Cherry Joe.**

Don't be afraid of the vodka. You use a very, very small amount for each

shake and it really does help to bring out those alcohol-soluble flavors. Besides...the kids'll sleep better. So might you.

CHERRY JOE

COURTESY OF WILES-SMITH DRUGS
MEMPHIS, TENNESSEE

✦ ✦

For the syrup:

2 cups water
10 ounces sugar
1½ teaspoons cherry flavoring
½ teaspoon red food coloring
2 teaspoons vodka

For the shake:

1 quart old-fashioned-style vanilla ice cream
¼ cup cherry syrup
¼ cup whole milk

OPPOSITE: Bear prepares to take his medicine: a Cherry Joe.
BELOW: If the Cherry Joe isn't to your liking, have the cherry ice cream soda.

Make the syrup: In a small saucepan over medium heat, combine the water and sugar and cook until the sugar is dissolved. Remove from the heat and stir in the cherry flavoring, food coloring, and vodka. Let the cherry syrup mixture cool completely before using. (This makes about 2½ cups syrup. Store leftover syrup, covered, in the refrigerator for up to 6 months.)

Make the shake: In a blender, combine the ice cream, the cherry syrup, and the milk. Blend until well combined. Do not overblend or the shake will be too thin. Divide between 2 glasses and serve immediately with straws.

YIELD: 2 SHAKES

Today the American road has no end; the road that went nowhere now goes everywhere.
HENRY FORD

✦ ✦ ✦ ✦ ✦ ✦ ✦ ✦ ✦ ✦

MELANIE'S SOUL FOOD, MEMPHIS, TENNESSEE
1215 HOURS

OPPOSITE: **Ms. Jimmie and her daughter Erika in the kitchen at Melanie's.**
BOTTOM LEFT: **Another soul survivor.**
BOTTOM RIGHT: **Jimmie's great-granddaughter, Tatyana.**

Walking into Melanie's Soul Food in north Memphis, I'm acutely aware of one thing: I'm white. The nice thing is that no one seems too shocked and no one seems to hold it against me. It's Saturday lunch rush, and there are plenty of folks queued up for the hot line. I peek over and around to see what's on the steam table, and all the greatest hits are there: sweet potatoes, greens, black-eyed peas, a couple different kinds of chicken, and a very alluring pan of what appear to be smoked turkey legs. I've got a straight-shot view back into the kitchen, and it takes a nanosecond to spot the ringleader, a stately woman in her...well, actually I can't tell how old she is, but I can tell that she's been around and she knows what she's doing and everyone else knows she's in charge. She's quietly giving instructions while stirring something. I breathe deeply, trying to suck in a whiff of the pot's steam, and I get it: chitlins—cleaned pig intestines, that is. Of course, depending on the region and the cook, the intestines in question may be large or small. My heart sinks because if there is one member of the soul food cast I don't dig, it's chitlins.

✦ ✦ ✦ ✦ ✦ ✦ ✦ ✦ ✦ ✦

I'm munching my turkey when a lively-looking waitress comes by to check on my satisfaction. After assuring her that I'm just getting warmed up, I ask her what soul food is. She is clearly taken aback. Only a white boy from the city would ask such a question, and I don't think many white city boys wander into Melanie's—though they would if they knew what was good for them.

"It's about people, I guess," she says with a smile, and leaves.

Maybe, but I think smoked turkey legs may have something to do with it, too.

I get to meet the matriarch of this operation, Ms. Jimmie, who turns out to be in her mid-sixties. She's a great-grandmother, and if I count her family members right they're all here today—most of them working. I ask Ms. Jimmie about her cooking, and you can tell it's not something she sits around pondering. She just does it the way her mother did it and her mother before her. She's proud of her place in the community—politicians and leaders come here. When I comment on the irony of the soulless needing soul food she chuckles, but only to humor me.

Then she talks about the chitlins. I come closer to the pot, even though my instincts tell me to head for the door. She tells me about all the soaking, the boiling, the draining, the rinsing, and I think about all this work just to produce something that by my reckoning is barely edible. But that's the nature of soul food: to elevate the meager into something whole and good, even if good still tastes kinda poopy to me. She tells me to go out to the dining room and she'll send out a plate. At least three sets of eyes turn to me. This is match point. Eat these and I'm in. Refuse and I'm just another pale poseur lookin' to gain the culinary street cred I have neither earned nor deserved.

Thank you, Ma'am.

I sit at a big booth and reach for a bottle of pepper sauce. I make every crew member I can find sit down with me.

The chitlins come on a big oval plate. They've been tossed with tiny pieces of chile and peppers. Without hesitation, I dig in. They are properly cooked, yielding yet firm. The heat of the chile balances the fatty edge that all intestines have no matter what you do. They are the best chitlins I have ever had, but no matter what I do I cannot make myself like them. It's the deep, primal, unmoveable gameyness of the aroma that gets me, and I wonder where this comes from. If I didn't know what they were, would I feel any different? Is it social stigma? I'm ashamed because I like to think I am without snobbery regarding food and I often brag that there is nothing that I will not eat. But there's just not enough tea on the table to wash down the rest of the chitlins. Luckily there is dessert: homemade cakes, cobblers, and a curious dish called butter roll, which is nothing more than bread dough in a loose custard. Of course, no one at Melanie's is about to give away any recipes. But I think I've come close to recreating two of the dishes I enjoyed there. If you want the real thing, you're going to have to make a trip to Memphis.

OPPOSITE: **Trinetra Leach serves up more swee'tea.** BELOW: **A pan of hot wings and, yes...a spaghetti sandwich.**

Every

time I ran across a dish built on a platform of smoked turkey legs, I ordered it. This dish is an amalgam of those experiences. Although I prefer my own seasoned salt blend, Lawry's brand is a pretty close second. As for the smoked turkey legs, they're available at most megamarts these days. And they're cheap, which is why so many restaurants in the South serve them.

BELOW: **Braised turkey leg, corn bread, peas and sweet potatoes. Everything a growing boy needs.**

MEMPHIS-STYLE TURKEY LEGS
INSPIRED BY A DISH AT MELANIE'S SOUL FOOD

✦ ✦

4 smoked turkey legs
1 tablespoon seasoned salt
1 cup hot barbecue sauce
1 tablespoon dark brown sugar
1 tablespoon freshly squeezed lemon juice

Preheat the oven to 450 degrees.

Place the legs in a 13-by-9-inch metal baking pan and sprinkle with the Season-All. Pour 1 cup of water into the bottom of the pan and cover tightly with aluminum foil. Bake on the middle rack of the oven for 1 hour. After 1 hour, gently uncover the pan and turn the legs over. Continue to bake for another hour. Remove from the oven and drain off any remaining water.

Combine the barbecue sauce, brown sugar, and lemon juice in a medium saucepan over high heat and bring to a boil. Remove from the heat and glaze the turkey legs with the sauce. Serve immediately.

YIELD: 4 SERVINGS

If you run into this dish (and it goes by many names) in a restaurant, odds are good that you are in the middle of nowhere. Originally cooked with dough left over from bread prepared for the slave master's table, we've adapted it for the modern larder. It's a cross between bread pudding and something kinda cobblerlike. Unique.

DOUGH PUDDING
INSPIRED BY A DESSERT AT MELANIE'S SOUL FOOD

✦ ✦

For the sauce:

> 1 (12-ounce) can evaporated milk
> 1 cup water
> ½ cup sugar
> 2 tablespoons unsalted butter
> ½ teaspoon vanilla extract
> ¼ teaspoon freshly grated nutmeg

For the dough:

> Dough for 1 (9-inch) pie
> 2 tablespoons sugar
> ¼ teaspoon ground cinnamon
> 2 tablespoons unsalted butter, cut into small pieces

Preheat the oven to 350 degrees.

Make the sauce: Combine the milk, water, sugar, butter, vanilla, and nutmeg in a medium saucepan over medium heat. Bring to a simmer and cook for 4 to 5 minutes. Set aside until ready to use.

Prepare the dough: Roll! the dough out on a lightly floured surface until ⅛ inch thick, in the shape of a square. Cut the dough into 8 even strips, then cut each strip in half crosswise. Evenly distribute the butter over the surface. Sprinkle the sugar and nutmeg on top. Roll each strip into a snail shape and lay in the bottom of a 9-inch-square glass baking dish.

Pour the sauce over the rolls and bake on the middle rack of the oven for 45 minutes, or until the top is well browned.

YIELD: 4 TO 6 SERVINGS

NOTEBOOK ENTRY

One of the things we hear over and over again from the cooks and especially the waitresses working in the small restaurants along the road is that they do it for the people. Sure, they need the money, but it's not the money that keeps them doing it. It's the people. Clearly, for these folks, the hospitality industry is still hos-

pitable. They give something of themselves with every meal they serve, and that also gives them a bit of ownership, which brings with it pride. And pride changes everything. Of course, hospitality is a two-way street. It's also about graciously receiving, and that is so not a part of the modern American mind-set.

Guest C
THANK YOU

TABLE NO. | PERSONS | SERVER

TAKE ME TO THE RIVER

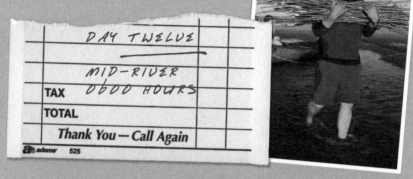

DAY TWELVE

MID-RIVER
TAX   0600 HOURS
TOTAL
Thank You — Call Again

adams   525

It's dawn and I'm on a large sandbar out in the middle of the Mississippi River, stuck in between Kentucky and Missouri. The sandbar doesn't have a name, which makes stating my position rather difficult, seeing as I left my GPS back on the bike, which is some five miles from here.

There is nothing here but sand and a sea of green willow, a sappy, weedy, canelike vegetation that apparently requires nothing but sand and water to live.

We spent the night here last night after canoeing two and a half hours to get here. This is a twisty section of river that actually flows north, so it felt like we were paddling against the current even though we weren't. Why canoes? Because I wanted to get on the river, where I could feel the cold of the water, watch the eddies and boils and cross-currents. I wanted to get a better look at the birds, to see fish jump, and, well, basically to get wet and not have to wear a helmet for a while. And I needed some decent exercise.

BELOW RIGHT:
I spend most of my afternoon cutting green willows for a grill. That's right, you can grill on wood as long as the wood is good and green.
BELOW LEFT: **Like a good conquistador of European descent, if I can't stay, I leave my mark.**
OPPOSITE: **Dutch oven paradise.**

We have a crew of three running this portion of the trip: John the skipper, Clayton the first mate, and Eli, who's kind of a mate's apprentice. I've been traveling in John's boat, the Ladybug. It's a massive thing, some 26½ feet long and 4½ feet wide, handmade down in Clarksdale, Mississippi, from cypress. The other two boats are fiberglass and aluminum, but hardy craft nonetheless. John is an accomplished riverman and looks like an Iron Man triathlon type, only with a ZZ Top beard. It balances the brim on his hat, which has to be at least twelve inches wide. We brought food with us and do all our cooking via campfire, most of it in Dutch ovens, including potatoes simmered in river water, mustard greens with onions, and corn. John brought both beef and pork steaks, which we grill on the aforementioned green willow saplings, which took about three hours to cut and trim. We spread out all the coals between two larger logs, then lay the saplings across just like a grill, only with very little room between the sticks. As soon as the meat goes on, the saplings begin to smoke and steam, but there is no out-and-out combustion until long after the steaks are cooked. The smoke infuses the meat perfectly. It is an old cooking method, of course. Christopher Columbus wrote of seeing natives in the

Unusual travel suggestions are dancing lessons from God.
KURT VONNEGUT

West Indies cooking meats and fish on saplings. They called it *barbacoa*. The word eventually became the source of both barbecue and buccaneer.

Last night would have been a great sleeping night, breezy and cool, but the moon was so bright on the sand you needed sunglasses, and despite the fact that the river's about half a mile across here, the barge traffic was so loud that when I did sleep I dreamt of street cleaners. Anyway, we're getting ready to row again. We've got about eight miles to our extraction point, and that will take some work because it's not just us, it's all this stupid film gear, including lights and a generator. And since Mike the sound man is loaded with gear, he can't row at all (audio guys are notoriously lazy).

RIGHT: **Nightfall.**
BELOW: **John and the Ladybug.**

✦ ✦ ✦ ✦ ✦ ✦ ✦ ✦ ✦ ✦

NEW MADRID, MISSOURI
1420 HOURS

I'm cruising down Mill Street in New Madrid (emphasis on the "ma") looking for yet another Jim's Café, long known for an item called the quake burger, a sandwich of mythic proportions named for the catastrophic series of earthquakes that struck this area in 1812. The main quake (which would have registered an 8.5 on the Richter scale if there'd been one back then) is the biggest in North America's recorded history and opened chasms in the earth so large that the river flowed upstream for nearly an hour just to fill them. I'm going about thirty down Mill Street and I've just decided to open my visor to better discern the aromas that I feel certain will guide me to Jim's when a big, juicy wasp smacks me in the face and wedges himself between my noggin and my helmet just off my right eye. By the time I stop the bike, get my gloves off, undo the helmet, and set the beastie free, he's nailed me four times. And he flies away, the fiend. I'm left holding my aching melon, which quickly swells to the point that I can't get the helmet on for another hour. While I'm sitting there wincing, a kid comes up and tells me that Jim's has been closed for over a year.

BELOW: **Nursing multiple wasp hits.**

Great. Ride on.

✦ ✦ ✦ ✦ ✦ ✦ ✦ ✦ ✦ ✦

DAY THIRTEEN
POPEYE STATUE, CHESTER, ILLINOIS
0812 HOURS

The middle Mississippi is marked by rolling bluffs on either side, some of which can get quite high. The bluffs are evidence of an older river that's had time to bed down into the land. The younger portion of the river, down south, hasn't had the necessary time to settle, and given its habit of flooding and shifting, it may never.

There's a nice view of the Chester Bridge here, and down to the left a small park commemorating Chester's most famous citizen, Popeye the Sailor. Okay, it's actually about Popeye creator Elzie Crisler Segar, but the bronze statue by the river is of Popeye. To honor this character's considerable culinary influence, we all open cans of spinach and dine al fresco. I have never eaten canned spinach before, and it's not bad. The only one who can't seem to get it down is J. C., but hey, he's French.

> Part of the secret of success in life is to eat what you like and let the food fight it out inside.
> MARK TWAIN

BELOW LEFT:
Chester's most famous product and the best celebrity endorsement a vegetable has ever had.
BELOW RIGHT: The Bridge on 51 outside Chester, Illinois.

You should, of course, serve this over yams because "I yam what I yam."

CREAMED SPINACH
ROAD INSPIRED

⬩ ⬩

2 pounds fresh spinach, rinsed and stemmed

2 tablespoons unsalted butter

½ cup chopped onion

1 teaspoon kosher salt

2 cloves garlic, minced

½ teaspoon freshly ground black pepper

½ teaspoon freshly grated nutmeg

½ cup heavy cream

1 teaspoon grated lemon zest

Bring a pot of salted water to a boil over high heat. Add the spinach and cook for 2 minutes. Pour into a fine-mesh strainer and run under cold water to help stop the cooking. Squeeze the spinach until absolutely all of the liquid is gone. Coarsely chop and set aside.

Place the butter in a 12-inch straight-sided sauté pan set over medium heat. Once the butter has melted, add the onion and salt and cook until the onion is translucent, 4 to 5 minutes. Add the garlic and continue to cook for another 2 to 3 minutes, making sure not to burn the garlic. Add the spinach, pepper, and nutmeg to the pan and stir just to heat through. Add the cream, stir to combine, and cook until the liquid has reduced and thickened slightly, 3 to 4 minutes. Remove from the heat, add the lemon zest, and stir to combine. Serve immediately.

YIELD: 4 SERVINGS

✦ ✦ ✦ ✦ ✦ ✦ ✦ ✦ ✦

ALTON'S VISITORS CENTER, ALTON, ILLINOIS
1310 HOURS

Alton, Illinois, is already a strange place for me to be since everything has my name on it. There are signs saying "Help Keep Alton Clean" and billboards for "Haunted Alton." I drop by the Alton Visitors Center to set the record straight on the pronunciation of the name. I tell them it's "Al-ton" but they say it's "All-ton." I counter with the argument that if that were true, the name Albert would be pronounced "All-burt." They don't care. Stubborn Midwesterners.

They are, however, nice enough to give me an Alton T-shirt and a nifty Alton toothpick dispenser. Oh, and a shirt with a picture of a man-eating Piasa Bird on it. That's the horrible, scaled creature with wings, deer antlers, and a lion's mane that Jacques Marquette saw painted on a bluff over the Mississippi around 1671 or some such thing. I ask the ladies at the Visitors Center if the Piasa is like a "liger," but they don't get it. After we tell them of our quest for road food, the ladies look straight at me and say in unison: "Fast Eddie's."

BELOW: Sinatra may have owned Vegas, but this...this is my town.

✦ ✦ ✦ ✦ ✦ ✦ ✦ ✦ ✦ ✦

FAST EDDIE'S BON AIR, ALTON, ILLINOIS
1447 HOURS

Located just off Broadway, Fast Eddie's is actually Fast Eddie's Bon Air. The Bon Air was built by Anheuser-Busch back in 1921 because the brewery wanted a bar. Problem was, in 1931 legislation was passed making it illegal for breweries to own bars. And so the Bon Air was sold to the Balaco family, who ran it for fifty years. In 1981 Eddie Sholar bought the place and converted it to the Fast Eddie's roadhouse concept.

ROADHOUSE. 1: An inn, usually outside the city limits, providing meals, dancing, liquor, and sometimes gambling.
2: A very bad Patrick Swayze movie.

BELOW: Today, Fast Eddie's sticks to its roadhouse roots. No one under 21 is allowed and all food must be consumed on premises. Although all the food is dang good, the house smoked brats are far and away the best thing on the menu, and at 99 cents they're stupid cheap. If I lived in Alton I would spend quite a bit of time at Fast Eddie's.

It's not an inn, but hey, how many bars do you know that rent rooms? Not a nice thought. Eddie's does food and drink and live music, but it's the mood that says roadhouse. Hand-painted signs, exclusive motorcycle parking. Even standing in the rain, I know that this is the real thing. As I approach the front entrance, the door swings open and issues forth old people. Lots of old people. A cushy van from the nearby seniors' home pulls up and fills up. I can't tell if they've been drinking, but they sure love the food. One lady in her mid-one-hundreds takes a liking to me and attempts to drag me onto the bus. This ticks off a man in his nineties, who starts hollerin' at me. I'm starting to think someone's heading home without his beer money.

Bear rescues me from the bus and gets me inside. Even in the middle of a workday afternoon, Eddie's is jumping. The customers are not a seedy lot, just regular folks and some bikers whose custom Harley-Davidsons we'd parked next to. We meet Eddie Jr., who's been running the place for the last few years, and he hooks us up with some chow. Here is the entire menu at Fast Eddie's:

◆ Big Elwood on a Stick $1.99 (marinated tenderloin)
◆ ½ pound Fat Eddie Burger $.99
◆ Homemade Bratwurst $.99
◆ Pork Kabobs $1.29
◆ Peel n Eat Shrimp $.29 Each
◆ Hot Chick on a Stick $2.99 (Cajun style)
◆ French Fries $.99 (a huge basket)

That's all there is, and here's the thing: it's good. In fact the brats are some of the best I've had, the burger is perfectly cooked, and the Hot Chick on a Stick revives my flagging faith in chicken wings. The only catch about the food at Eddie's is that you can't take it to go. There is no actual drink minimum, but obviously the intent is that you do so. Eddie can't stay in business selling half-pound burgers for a buck. And you have to be twenty-one to even set foot in the place. Oh well, guess you can always lock the kids in the car if you crack a window.

Before leaving, I have a talk with Eddie, and what I admire most is that he knows what the place is and doesn't want to mess with it. He tells me that he fends off franchise and chain offers at least once a week. I can understand why. It's a great concept and I could probably open three in Atlanta and retire. But he won't do that. And I love him for it.

OPPOSITE: **Roadhouse art at Fast Eddie's.**

HOT CHICK ON A STICK

COURTESY OF FAST EDDIE'S BON AIR
ALTON, ILLINOIS

✦ ✦

16 chicken drummettes (about 2 pounds)
1 teaspoon seasoned salt (homemade or Lawry's)
1 teaspoon Cajun seasoning (like Emeril's or one of your choice)

Preheat the oven to 450 degrees.

Place the chicken drummettes in a large mixing bowl, add the seasonings, and toss to coat well. Place the drummettes on 4 kebab skewers. Lay the skewers on a half sheet pan lined with parchment paper. Bake on the middle rack of the oven for 45 minutes. Place the skewers in the refrigerator until cold, at least 1 hour.

When ready to serve, preheat a grill to 350 degrees.

Remove the chicken from the refrigerator and place on the grill. Cook for 5 minutes per side. Serve immediately.

YIELD: 4 APPETIZER SERVINGS

RIGHT: **Pondering the viability of my diet program.**
BELOW: **Angela and Christine on the hot line.**
OPPOSITE: **Hot Chicks on a Stick and a housemade brat.**

✦ ✦ ✦ ✦ ✦ ✦ ✦ ✦ ✦

DAY FOURTEEN
ON THE MISSISSIPPI, HEADING TO PADUCAH FROM UNION CITY
1050 HOURS

I'm dictating this into my iPod because both hands are a little busy. I'm attempting to pilot the Susan L. Stall, a six-thousand-horsepower twin-screw towboat built in 1976. I'm looking out at a quarter mile of barges lashed together in front of her, twenty-seven barges in all, containing everything from chloroform to iron ore to something called pet coke, which I understand has something to do with petroleum processing and burns quite nicely in power plants. Each one of these barges weighs something on the order of fourteen hundred tons, and we are pushing the whole enchilada upriver to Paducah, and to tell you the truth, I'm not even sure what state that's in. Kentucky, I think.

> A ship in harbor is safe—but that is not what ships are for.
> JOHN A. SHEDD

Nine crew members work six-hour shifts keeping the Susan L. Stall going. And one cook keeps them going: Kathryn Williamson. She has been cooking on boats owned by the Canal Barge Company for seventeen years, but she's planning on retiring at the end of this trip. A trip for these guys is twenty-eight days. You don't leave the boat once you're on board. Everything is brought to you from shore. We

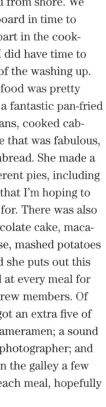

RIGHT: Athough they appear to eat constantly, the crew of the Susan L. Stall are mostly rail thin. That's because they actually work... constantly. The crew toils in twenty-eight-day "trips," during which time they work six hours on six hours off. They never, ever leave the boat. OPPOSITE: Ms. Kathryn and one of her many desserts, a coconut cream pie, aboard the Susan L. Stall.

didn't get on board in time to actually take part in the cooking, although I did have time to do a good bit of the washing up. But Kathryn's food was pretty great. She did a fantastic pan-fried pork chop, beans, cooked cabbage, dirty rice that was fabulous, rolls, and cornbread. She made a couple of different pies, including a coconut pie that I'm hoping to get the recipe for. There was also a German chocolate cake, macaroni and cheese, mashed potatoes and gravy. And she puts out this kind of spread at every meal for just the nine crew members. Of course, she's got an extra five of us now: two cameramen; a sound guy; J. C., the photographer; and me. So I'll be in the galley a few hours before each meal, hopefully

learning some of her secrets before she retires. I'm told that when we start dinner at three o'clock, I'll be working on chicken 'n' dumplings. I'm hoping to get the recipe, because it's famous up and down this part of the river.

You know, being on a towboat is kind of like being on a steam-powered paddleboat back in the 1800s. These are the boats that do most of the work of the river, pushing goods upstream and downstream, day and night, 365 days a year. If Mark Twain was alive today he'd be piloting one of these things. Of course, it's heavy work, much of the day spent doing either maintenance on the boat itself or checking the lashings, the steel cables that hold all of the barges together into one boat. It's a quarter mile from the wheelhouse to the front of the boat. I've hiked out there. I actually got to climb down on one of the inner walls of the barges to check for water, all the way out to the head, where if one were to fall over, one would be dead, no question about it. A quarter mile of boat is just absolutely amazing to watch in action; you get to see the river from a completely

BELOW: **Life on the Susan L. Stall.**

different perspective. We saw a lot of the river on the canoe trip, of course, but we're covering a lot more territory here, seeing a lot more of the way the river works—the navigation. We learned that southbound vessels have the right-of-way, which makes sense. If we're in a bend and meet a boat, we often have to stop and let that boat go by. When you're a quarter mile long, it's hard to take a turn, and the navigation system up on the bridge actually shows projections three minutes in advance, which is when you have to make your course adjustments.

The people on the boat are nice, incredibly polite. When the crew comes in for their lunch meal, every one of the crew members hangs his hat on a peg on the wall, because you wouldn't dare sit down at Miss Kathryn's table with a hat on your head. Everybody carries his plate to the sink. The guys are rough and tumble, that's for sure, but there's something genuine about them that strikes me as part of a forgotten America, something you don't see much of anymore. As for Miss Kathryn, I know her breed of cook is almost gone.

BELOW: Message board on our tug... and perhaps the best words to live by that I have ever seen.

125

Neither Miss Kathryn nor I wrote anything down, but this comes close to what we served on the boat. If you're like me, you'll double the pepper at the last minute.

CHICKEN-'N'-DUMPLINGS
INSPIRED BY THOSE SERVED ON THE SUSAN L. STALL CANAL BARGE
HICKMAN, KENTUCKY

◆ ◆

3 cups all-purpose flour, plus about 1 cup for rolling
11 ounces whole milk
1½ teaspoons baking powder
1 teaspoon salt
4 quarts chicken broth or stock
Meat from 1 roasted or rotisserie chicken, skin discarded
1 teaspoon freshly ground black pepper

BELOW: Another satisfied customer.

Place the flour, milk, baking powder, and salt in the bowl of a stand mixer. Stir just until the dough begins to come together. Using the paddle attachment, mix on medium speed for 1 minute. Cover the bowl with a tea towel and let sit at room temperature for 5 to 10 minutes.

Place the broth in an 8-quart pot over medium heat and bring to a rolling boil.

Lay down two large pieces of parchment or freezer paper and tape them to the counter. Generously sprinkle the surface with flour, at least 1 cup. Divide the dough in half. Roll one half of the dough ⅛ to ¼ inch thick, generously sprinkling more flour onto the dough so that it is well coated. Slice the dough into 1-inch-wide strips and then into 1-inch squares. Set the dumplings aside on a sheet pan. Repeat with the second half of the dough.

When all of the dumplings are cut, gently drop them into the boiling broth, a handful at a time. Once all of the dumplings have been added, cook for 35 minutes at a gentle simmer, stirring occasionally. After the sauce has thickened well, add the chicken and pepper and stir to combine. Continue to cook for another 5 minutes, or just until the meat is heated through. Serve immediately.

YIELD: 10 TO 12 SERVINGS

✦ ✦ ✦ ✦ ✦ ✦ ✦ ✦ ✦ ✦

DAY FIFTEEN
PRINCE PIT BBQ, BARDWELL, KENTUCKY
1415 HOURS

Prince Pit BBQ on Highway 51 is everything I want in a barbecue joint, meaning not much. On one side of the gravel lot there is an old concession trailer converted into a serving stand, a picnic table, and a Coke machine. Beyond that is a small travel trailer and a ramshackle tent made of metal fence, sheet plastic, and tarpaulins. Inside this stands a row of massive smokers. I watch as Ricky Prince loads the smokers with hams and shoulders. (I've always preferred ham to shoulder for barbecue, but I know I'm in the minority.) What's most interesting, though, is that this is the one day a week Mr. Prince smokes up several sides of mutton. Mutton is sheep that's more than a year old. It's very difficult to get in this country, but Mr. Prince has a source. It's early in the afternoon and these beasts won't be ready till morning, but when they are folks will be waiting. By 9 a.m., in fact, all the mutton will be gone. I want some of this mutton very badly and consider waiting it

BELOW: **Ricky Prince outside his shop in Bardwell, Kentucky.**

out. But we've only been back on the road from our river excursion for a couple of hours and we need to roll. Luckily, there's enough of today's Q to feed us, along with the standard fixin's (which are anything but standard—they're far better). Dining at the picnic table, we witness the same scene over and over. A car or truck crunches onto the gravel. The occupant, a desperate look in his or her eye, hurries to the stand, only to be met by Ricky's shaking head. There'll be no more Q today. Dejected, the seekers lumber back to their vehicles, shooting us reproachful, even hateful looks. The desires of our coterie have thrown off the local people-to-meat ratio. We are dining on the Q of others. There's just not enough to go around. But the way I look at it, tomorrow morning I'll be at least a hundred miles gone and these people will be eating smoked mutton. So who's the winner?

BELOW RIGHT: Ricky Prince with his wood fire pit. This is serious Q.

Barbecue

Barbecue enthusiasts often go too far with their sauces, creating so many layers of flavor that the end result tastes like liquidized tower of Babel. At Prince Pit BBQ they keep it straightforward and simple. I like that. This is a big batch, I'll grant you, but if you keep it in the fridge it will last a very long time. Oh, and it's good on scrambled eggs.

HOME VERSION OF PRINCE PIT BBQ HAM AND SAUCE

COURTESY OF PRINCE PIT BBQ
BARDWELL, KENTUCKY

✦ ✦ ✦ ✦ ✦ ✦ ✦ ✦ ✦ ✦ ✦ ✦ ✦ ✦) ✦ ✦ ✦ ✦ ✦ ✦ ✦ ✦ ✦ ✦ ✦

For the barbecue sauce:

> **32 ounces tomato ketchup**
> **48 ounces white vinegar**
> **8 ounces light brown sugar**
> **½ ounce ground cayenne**
> **¼ ounce red pepper flakes**

For the ham:

> **1 (18- to 24-pound) fully cooked bone-in ham, preferably Fieldstone brand**

Make the sauce: Combine all the ingredients in a large stainless-steel pot. Stir and place over medium heat. Bring to a simmer, then reduce the heat to low. Simmer for 1 hour. Let the sauce cool, then pour it into a clean container with a lid. Store in the refrigerator until ready to use. This yields about 3 quarts of sauce.

Make the ham: Prepare a smoking pit with hickory coals and preheat to 190 to 200 degrees. Lay the ham over the smoking pit, making sure the meat is at least 32 inches from the hickory coals. Smoke the ham at 190 to 200 degrees for 12 to 14 hours. Baste the meat every 3 hours with barbecue sauce.

YIELD: 30 TO 40 SERVINGS

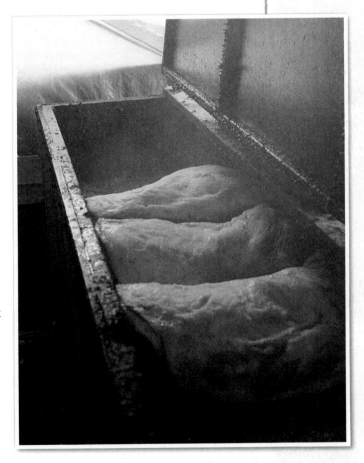

BELOW: The famed smoked mutton at Prince Pit BBQ. Ricky Prince smokes these Friday for sale Saturday morning. He says that by 9 a.m., it's all gone. I consider staying for the feed fest but we have to make tracks.

♦ ♦ ♦ ♦ ♦ ♦ ♦ ♦ ♦ ♦

DAY SIXTEEN
ST. LOUIS, MISSOURI
0822 HOURS

BELOW: To some, St. Louis means beer. To others, barbecue. To me and many natives of the city, St. Louis means donuts.
OPPOSITE: The goods at Donut Drive-In.

I had been worried about how to handle St. Louis. We'd been through last year on our east-west journey and spent some time pondering the famed 1904 World's Fair, which turned out to be one of the pivotal food events in U.S. history. And we'd munched frozen custard concretes at Ted Drewes'. But in Memphis, and then again at a fuel stop in Kentucky, St. Louis natives and locals mentioned their fondness for local donuts. When we got to town late on a Friday night, Mark jumped on the internet and with a little triangulating found a dense concentration of donut shops in southwest St. Louis. Checking the map, we saw that there were five all within a two-mile radius. This merited investigation.

Although we experience a great many definitive donut moments this morning, the jewels in our deep-fried and glazed crown are the offerings from World's Fair Donuts on Vandeventer. It is not that the donuts are necessarily better than those at Donut Drive-In on Chippewa or those at St. Louis Hills Donut Shop on Hampton; it's just that everything about World's Fair smacks of an age gone by.

The World's Fair shop, which sits on a prominent corner in a neighborhood that looks like it's gone from good to bad to gentrified to arty, is small. It's manned, even on Saturday morning, by none other than Terry and Peggy Clanton, who purchased it back in 1976. Each day since, with the exception of the seven major holidays (Christmas, Easter, Independence Day, Labor Day, Memorial Day, Thanksgiving, and New Year's Day), Mr. Clanton makes the donuts and Mrs. Clanton sells 'em.

When we arrive, there is a friendly line out the door. Being a food quasi-celebrity and therefore special, I push my way into the store to announce that we have come to elevate their quaint shop into the stratum of national phenomenon. Mrs. Clanton, hands flying to fill boxes and make change via a 1950s

OPPOSITE TOP: Terry
Clanton makes the
donuts.
OPPOSITE BOTTOM:
Peggy Clanton sells
the donuts.

cash register, couldn't care less. She doesn't have time for my foolishness because she has her customers to take care of. Having been put firmly in my place, I go back and make Brett stand in line while I go around to the side window to watch Mr. Clanton do some glazing. In contrast to his wife's hummingbird-like gesticulations, Mr. Clanton is slow, smooth, and efficient. A terrapin, if you like, who knows all too well that not all food is fast. Near as I can tell, he makes every single donut this shop sells, and each bears the sign of craftsmanship. The old-fashioneds are especially artful. I take a bite and at first it seems too simple, even plain...like it might be missing something. There is no glaze, but as I chew, the crunchy, almost hushpuppy-like exterior blends with the yielding interior. Sweetness emerges, then hides again, and I realize that there is a great deal going on here if I'll only take the time to taste it. I look around at others who are eating their donuts on the street and I notice something funny. We're all eating like Mr. Clanton moves—slowly, but with purpose. That's not something you see much of in America. Speed is our mantra, and most of our food is designed to be tasted quickly, swallowed, forgotten. But the donuts at World's Fair slow things down. I catch the eye of several locals, who smile at me through crumbs. For many of the locals standing around munching with me, this is a weekly ritual, and rituals are not to be trifled with. I finish my donut, drop and do twenty push-ups, roll over and do twenty sit-ups. Good. Now there's room for more donuts.

So what makes St. Louis donuts so darned good? Well, all these shops do have three things in common:

1. They're family owned.
2. The donuts are handmade on site.
3. They all entertain a demanding clientele.

This last piece is an important one. Regulars keep you honest. They resist change, and if you let the quality slip they'll burn you down and out. But if you keep up your game they will be loyal, working like antibodies to resist the incursion of national chains, which would only ruin everything for everybody.

Are donuts road food? If we're to believe the legends, the donut was invented by Hanson Crocket Gregory, an American sea captain who, when caught in a sudden squall, put the Danish olycake he'd been munching on standby by sticking it on one of the pegs of the ship's wheel. If this tale be true, then donuts were born of travel and therefore qualify, without question.

✦ ✦ ✦ ✦ ✦ ✦ ✦ ✦ ✦

DAY SEVENTEEN
MONROE CITY, NORTHERN MISSOURI
0750 HOURS

OPPOSITE: Coffee in
the Rebel camp.
BELOW: Hash browns
and pancakes in the
Union camp.

Traveling through Missouri, we catch wind of a Civil War battle reenactment being staged in Monroe City. Hoping for a taste of period chow, we decide to investigate. It's a cold and dreary dawn when we arrive, and we stop between the two camps to brew ourselves some coffee. That gets me to wondering about Civil War–era Joe.

The importance of coffee to both Union and Rebel troops has been well documented. Green coffee beans were the foot soldier's most precious expendable, even more precious than food. When the quartermaster supplied a division, company, or whatever group with coffee, this is what they'd do: a rubber blanket was laid on the ground and the beans would be carefully and evenly divided into small mounds, one for each soldier. Then the group's sergeant would take a copy of the roll call and turn around so he could not see the coffee. An assistant would point to one of the piles and say, "Sergeant, who gets this pile?" And the sergeant would read a name. Thus each pile of coffee beans would be distributed. Some men chose to roast their beans separately, but often the members of a mess (a small group of men who shared food rations and cooking duties) would pool their coffee and roast the beans in a pan over the fire. Rifle butts usually did the grinding. And hardtack was the preferred accompaniment.

After downing our own coffee, we move from camp to camp, starting with the Confederate side of the field, where morale this morning seems low following an evening of revelry. The coffee is wretched, tasting of socks at one fire and of sticks at another. The Confederates do receive points for authenticity, though. The clothing, weapons, tents— everything looks period to me, as do the messes themselves. Breakfast is being cooked on iron grates, and coffee boils in tin pots. Still awful, though. The Union camp proves a bit neater: There are more uniforms, and the coffee actually has coffee in it. But the jig is up when I open one pot to find...coffee bags! I didn't even know such a thing still existed. I chide the cook for destroying the nineteenth-century verisimilitude with a low-class culinary crutch. She throws a spoon at me, but luckily I escape unscathed. I move to another fire where an accomplished cook, the wife of one of the Union captains, has spit-roasted a wild goose, which is very nice indeed.

After breakfast, things get nasty, just as they did on July 10, 1861, when secessionist troops under Brigadier General Harris clashed rather haphazardly with Union forces under one Colonel Smith. I notice that the troops are so heavily caffeinated that when shot they don't even fall down. We consider taking the field with our iron horses but decide that would fly in the face of tradition, so we quietly turn north to do battle with our growing hunger.

We did not encounter rabbit stew on the road, but several of the Civil War reenactors at Monroe City spoke of it as standard fare for soldiers on both sides of the conflict. As soon as I got home I shot me a rabbit and threw this together.*

RABBIT STEW
INSPIRED BY MONROE CITY REENACTMENT
MONROE CITY, MISSOURI

✦ ✦

1 rabbit, about 3 pounds, cut up
½ cup all-purpose flour
1 tablespoon kosher salt
1 teaspoon freshly ground black pepper
4 tablespoons unsalted butter
2 medium onions, sliced
2 cups chopped waxy potatoes
2 cups chicken broth
1 cup white wine
2 tablespoons chopped fresh herbs, such as thyme, oregano, or parsley, divided

Toss the rabbit pieces in the flour and salt and pepper.

Place a 12-inch cast-iron skillet over medium heat, add the butter, and melt. Once the butter has melted, add the rabbit and brown on all sides, about 15 minutes. Add the onions, potatoes, broth, wine, and half of the herbs. Cover and bring to a simmer. Cook the rabbit for 25 minutes, then uncover and cook for another 10 minutes. Remove from the heat, sprinkle on the remaining herbs, and serve immediately.

YIELD: 4 TO 6 SERVINGS

*Okay, I didn't shoot it. I would have, but I feared being disowned by my daughter for taking out Thumper.

Guest Check

TABLE NO.	PERSONS	SERVER NO.	CHECK NO.
			8624 — 2

BEV • APPET • SOUP/SALAD • ENTREE • VEG • DESSERT

DAY SEVENTEEN

Hannibal, Missouri
0900 HOURS

We get to Hannibal, home of Mark Twain, early enough for me to find a church. I haven't been since the trip started and I need to get me some religion. I settle on a Presbyterian service at 10 a.m. and grab a pew in the back.

The sermon is from Romans, which is fine by me. Paul was quite a road man himself, and I find myself wondering what kind of bike he would have ridden.

I can't help but see him on a 1938 Matchless Clubman. Of course, if Timothy were with him there might have been a sidecar, but that would have slowed their frequent escapes. No, Timothy would have had his own ride, something Italian perhaps.

Hannibal is a nice town, but as soon as I start walking around I sense a problem. The Civil War folks talked to the local paper, which ran a story about our being in the area. Now fans are trickling in to seek us out. By the time I get to the hotel, people are waiting to catch me in the lobby. They've actually got the bikes staked out like paparazzi. A couple hours later, I realize I will have to make a break for it. It's not that I don't appreciate my fans, but I'm in road mode and need a little more space than Hannibal can provide. I make a break for the next town north, Quincy, and stumble into a jewel...make that two.

By the time we stopped at this truck stop in Taylor, Missouri, breakfast time was long past. But the nice thing about truck stops is that breakfast is never over. Where there are trucks, there are biscuits, and more often than not that means gravy. If you stop at the 18 Wheeler (and I suggest that you do), this is the gravy you'll get.

BELOW: **Hanging with a fellow road warrior at the 18 Wheeler.**

SAUSAGE GRAVY

COURTESY OF THE 18 WHEELER RESTAURANT
TAYLOR, MISSOURI

+ +

½ **pound bulk sausage, crumbled**
6 **tablespoons vegetable oil**
1 **teaspoon salt**
1 **teaspoon white pepper**
¾ **cup all-purpose flour**
5 **cups whole milk, divided**

Place the sausage, oil, salt, and white pepper in a 12-inch cast-iron skillet over medium heat. Cook until the sausage is done, 3 to 5 minutes, breaking it up into pieces until the sausage is in ½-inch chunks.

Add half the flour and stir until incorporated. Add the rest of the flour and stir again until it is all incorporated. Reduce the heat to medium-low. Cook, stirring occasionally, for 5 to 7 minutes, until the roux is just beginning to brown.

While the sausage mixture is cooking, heat 2 cups of the milk in a small saucepan over medium-low heat. Do not let it boil.

Once the sausage mixture has cooked, add the 3 cups cold milk all at once, whisking to break up the flour. Whisk continuously until the gravy thickens. Once the gravy begins to thicken, add half of the heated milk, whisking until it begins to thicken again. Add the remaining warm milk and whisk to combine. Turn the heat off and let the gravy sit for 5 minutes, stirring occasionally. Serve immediately.

YIELD: 6 CUPS, OR 4 TO 6 SERVINGS

✦ ✦ ✦ ✦ ✦ ✦ ✦ ✦ ✦

DAY EIGHTEEN
MAID-RITE SANDWICH SHOP, QUINCY, ILLINOIS
1322 HOURS

Standing outside the Maid-Rite Sandwich Shop on North 12th Street, I feel a great deal of satisfaction. This is exactly the kind of place that I was afraid didn't exist anymore. The Maid-Rite was one of the first franchises, and although it nearly became extinct in the 1990s, some say that it's on its way back here in the Midwest where it was born. Now, the Maid-Rite sandwich is a thing of legend. It is essentially a sloppy joe without any tomato product. No...that's wrong. The Maid-Rite is much finer in texture. The meat is ground so fine, in fact, that it's mousselike. This meat is seasoned with onions and sometimes a bit of mustard. but it's kept subtle. The mixture is sort of mashed into a bun like a reconstructed burger.

MAID RITE
SUPER MAID RITE
CHEESE RITE
SUPER CHEESE RITE
ROASTBEEF
SUPER ROASTBEEF
BAR-B-Q BEEF
SUPER BAR-B Q BEEF
TENDERLOIN
DOUBLE TENDERLOIN
STRIP TENDERLOIN
Dr Pepper

BELOW: A scene from the Maid-Rite Sandwich Shop in Quincy, Illinois.

143

This family-owned and -operated restaurant has been at it for over seventy years. And it's such a busy place that there needs to be one guy just for beverages (including the best cherry Coke I've ever had, made with homemade syrup), a lady just for pie (by law, all Midwestern restaurants must offer a minimum of five pies), a lady just for tenderloin sandwiches, and a squad for Maid-Rites. I wish to learn the craft of Maid-Rite assembly, so I press myself into the service of Mary Favre, who has been working here (and loving it) for thirty-five years. She tells me to wash my hands, which I do as quickly and as thoroughly as I can.

There is a vat of bubbling meat before us, and my job is to hold both pieces of a bun in one hand, then sweep down into the vat with a short metal spatula with the other, loading said spat with just enough meat to fill the sandwich, which will be weighed to ensure consistency. The tricky part is getting the meat onto the bun without getting it on your hands. This is much harder than it looks, and my clumsiness is rewarded with a smart scalding. Mary is patient, though, and by my fifth sandwich I'm showing signs of improvement.

ABOVE: The original soda fountain at Maid-Rite.

As I'm working, something about the sound from the dining area grabs my attention. It's the voices. It sounds like a big dinner party out there, everyone talking to everyone else. The sense of community in the Maid-Rite shop is palpable and it makes me feel all warm and fuzzy.

I ask Mary what it's like working with kids these days and she shakes her head. Like many small-town schoolteachers, she's trained generations here. She points out one particular girl, probably seventeen, whose mother had worked here at the same age. This one's a good one, says Mary, but kids today don't have to work for things the way they once did, so they don't really value jobs anymore. If they get tired or bored, they quit. I remind her that the food industry is not known for long-term employment, but she quickly corrects me by pointing out various staff members who have all been at Maid-Rite for over twenty-five years. When I ask her why, her answer is simple: "It's a family."

This sandwich appears in myriad forms throughout the Midwest, especially in Iowa and Illinois. Part hamburger, part sloppy joe, it defies description but is darned good.

LOOSE MEAT SANDWICH
ROAD INSPIRED

♦ ♦

1½ pounds ground beef

1 medium onion, very finely minced
   (This is important: a fine chop won't do. But don't be tempted
   to use a food processor or you'll end up with a watery mess.)

1 tablespoon prepared mustard

½ cup water

1 tablespoon Worcestershire sauce

¼ teaspoon kosher salt

Place the beef and onion in a 4-quart saucepan over medium heat. Cook until the beef is completely cooked through but not browning, 8 to 9 minutes, constantly mashing the beef with a potato masher in order to break the pieces into the smallest possible. Add the remaining ingredients and continue to simmer for another 15 minutes. Remove from the heat. Using a hand mixer, mix for another 2 to 3 minutes on high. Serve on hamburger buns with ketchup, mustard, cheese, and pickles.

YIELD: 6 SANDWICHES

BELOW: Mary Favre, a Maid-Rite veteran of thirty-plus years, shows me how to make a Maid-Rite sandwich. After a couple of disasters I start to get the hang of it.

You can find your way across this country using burger joints the way a navigator uses stars.

CHARLES KURALT

Needless to say, while riding upriver a guy has plenty of opportunity to lock jaw on catfish. I think this is the best of the bunch.

FRIED CATFISH
COURTESY OF FIN INN
GRAFTON, ILLINOIS

✦ ✦

8 (7- to 9-ounce) river catfish, gutted, head removed, and skinned

9 ounces cornmeal (about 1½ cups)

4½ ounces all-purpose flour (about ⅔ cup)

2 tablespoons Lawry's Seasoned Salt

1 tablespoon plus 1 teaspoon garlic powder

2 teaspoons freshly ground black pepper

1 cup whole milk

1 cup buttermilk

Peanut oil for frying

Fill a 10- to 12-quart cast-iron Dutch oven half full with peanut oil. Set over medium heat and bring the oil to 350 degrees.

Thoroughly rinse the catfish, pat dry, and set aside in the refrigerator until ready to fry.

In a large bowl, combine the cornmeal, flour, seasoned salt, garlic powder, and pepper. In a second bowl, combine the milk and buttermilk.

Dip the catfish one at a time into the milk mixture and then dredge in the cornmeal mixture. Gently lower the catfish into the oil and fry until the fish floats to the top of the oil and is golden brown, 3 to 4 minutes. Transfer to a cooling rack set in a half sheet pan and let cool for at least 5 minutes before serving.

YIELD: 4 SERVINGS

BELOW: Fishtanks line the walls of the Fin Inn. So don't order the catfish unless you don't mind being watched by one.

✦ ✦ ✦ ✦ ✦ ✦ ✦ ✦ ✦

DAY NINETEEN
BAXTER'S VINEYARDS, NAUVOO, ILLINOIS
1000 HOURS

I'm sitting in the gravel in the shade of an old bar here at Baxter's Vineyards, which makes old Nauvoo wine, here in Nauvoo, Illinois. Although Nauvoo may be best known as the home of the Mormon Church, not exactly a wine-drinking group, following the great Mormon exodus of 1846 the French Icarians moved in to set up what they hoped would be a social utopia. They brought considerable wine-making skills with them, and Nauvoo was a major wine region right up to Prohibition. The wines made here are unlike anything else bottled in America because the grapes are all either American natives or hybrids developed with French varieties over 150 years ago. My favorite offering is actually the Concord grape juice, which is fresh, crisp, tart, and one of the top five beverages I have ever enjoyed.

RIGHT: The winery's matriarch, Julia Pezley.
BELOW: American wines from American grapes at Baxter's in Nauvoo. Since I was riding I didn't partake, but I can vouch for the Concord grape juice, which was amazing.

Although the vineyards are picturesque, I won't lie to you. We're really here for Carol's Pies. We heard about pie lady Carol Sherrill when we were in town and came out to the vineyard to check out her skills. She serves us apple and rhubarb-strawberry, which is usually the first pie of the spring because strawberries and rhubarb are the first spring crops available. The pies are amazing, but instead of taking the credit Carol claims that her fifty-year-old converted pizza oven is the real miracle worker.

Nauvoo is also known for a distinctive blue cheese that used to age alongside the wine in local caves. They still serve it with apple pie here, but it's too salty for my taste. Besides, the creamery made Nauvoo Blue shut down a few years ago. Now the stuff is imported from who knows where and the Nauvoo label is stuck on it. Ick.

LEFT: Although Nauvoo no longer makes blue cheese, it's still a big seller here. **BELOW:** Carol (on the left in the V-neck) gives me the lowdown on the pies that are her life's work.

The fact that rhubarb and strawberries ripen together in early spring is all the proof I need that there is a God and that he loves us.

STRAWBERRY-RHUBARB PIE
BASED ON A RECIPE FROM CAROL'S PIES
NAUVOO, ILLINOIS

✦ ✦

For the crust:

10½ ounces all-purpose flour (about 2 cups)

5⅜ ounces chilled vegetable shortening (about ¾ cup)

¼ cup water

1 teaspoon table salt

One ice cube

2 tablespoons whole milk

1 tablespoon sugar

For the filling:

10½ ounces sugar (about 1½ cups)

2 tablespoons all-purpose flour

¼ teaspoon kosher salt

2 tablespoons unsalted butter, melted

1 whole egg

3 cups chopped fresh rhubarb

1 cup sliced strawberries

BELOW LEFT: **Baked goods at the Nauvoo Winery.**

Preheat the oven to 350 degrees.

Make the crust: Place the flour and shortening in a bowl and mix together using your fingers until the mixture is in pea-size pieces. In a small bowl, mix together the water and the salt until the salt is completely dissolved. Add the ice cube and stir until melted. Sprinkle the water, a little at a time, into the flour and shortening mixture until a dough forms. Divide the dough in half and shape it into two disks; wrap in plastic wrap and chill in the refrigerator for 30 minutes.

Roll out one of the dough disks between two sheets of parchment paper until large enough to cover the bottom and sides of a 9-inch pie pan. Place the dough in the bottom of the pan. Roll out the other disk in the same way, then cut into ½-inch-wide strips. Set both the dough-lined pan and the dough strips in the refrigerator while you make the filling.

Make the filling: In the bowl of a stand mixer with the whisk attachment, mix together the sugar, flour, salt, butter, and egg until light and creamy, about 1 minute. Add the rhubarb and strawberries and stir to combine.

Assemble the pie: Pour the filling into the pie pan lined with the dough and top with the dough strips, criss-crossing them to create a lattice effect. Brush the top crust with the milk, then sprinkle with the sugar. Bake on the middle rack of the oven until golden brown and bubbling, about 1 hour and 15 minutes. Let cool completely before slicing and serving.

YIELD: 1 (9-INCH) PIE

ABOVE: Although I kinda like it when the fruity filling blows out a little, you can use a pie bird if you don't.

✦ ✦ ✦ ✦ ✦ ✦ ✦ ✦ ✦

QUALITY FISHERIES, NIOTA, ILLINOIS
1121 HOURS

OPPOSITE TOP: Kirby Marsden, owner of Quality Fisheries. He's also president of the Illinois Commercial Fishing Association. And he knows his way around a smoker.
OPPOSITE BOTTOM: Smoked spoonbill, a cousin of the sturgeon, at Quality Fisheries.
BELOW: Nothing says "authentic" quite like a professionally hand-painted sign. Heck, anybody can print out a banner at Kinko's. But this took time and talent.

Not too far out of Nauvoo, we hit a small town called Niota. The first thing I notice coming around this little bend is a sign with a big fish wearing a top hat on it. Above the joyful fish (a channel cat, I believe), it says, "Quality Fisheries Smoked Fish." I lay on the brakes and feel the ABS pulsing, keeping the rear tire from locking up. Now, this is the first smoked fish I've seen on the trip, and it's an important indicator, because down in the South we save our smoke for pigs. But as you move higher into the Midwest, it's for fish. So clearly we've crossed that line. We go in and meet the owner, Kirby Marsden, who gives us a peek into the small operation. There are a lot of people with knives flying in the back and a lot of fish coming in the back door, some of which are still twitching as they hit the cutting board. (Now that's fresh.) The cutters work expertly, fabricating cuts for restaurants as far away as Chicago. Although some fresh fish is offered behind the refrigerated counter up front, most of it is smoked. There's smoked shovelnose sturgeon, smoked carp, smoked catfish. I'm in heaven.

After a little more conversation, we learn that Kirby is also the president of the Illinois Commercial Fishing Association and a true expert on the subject of fish. When questioned as to why his operation is based in this small town, he points to the river not a hundred yards away and explains that this is one of the healthiest fisheries along the entire river. I walk down and it's truly pristine. The water is clear and you can see fish everywhere.

Fresh Fish

	PER	POUND
Dressed Catfish	$2.	09#
Steaked Catfish (trimmed free of charge)	$2.	09#
Flathead Catfish Nuggets or	$2.	75#
Catfish fillets (no bones)	$3.	25#
Scored Carp	$1.	65#
Whole Dressed CARP	1.	00#
Scored Buffalo	1.	95
Whole Dressed Buffalo	1.	30#
Perch fillets	2.	25
Whole Dressed Perch	1.	25
Whole Dressed Flathead	$1.	69#
SPOONBILL fillets	2.	50#

Although a great majority of the Big Muddy is just that, muddy, here the water looks so good I want to drink it. But since the fish go in it, I don't.

Back at the shop we dine and compare. The sturgeon is strong and crumbly, perfect for working into a dip but not so good for out-of-hand eating. The catfish is much smoother, but my favorite is the carp, which has enough flavor to stand up to the smoke.

Just before we leave, we spy a handwritten paper sign that simply says "mushrooms." We ask Kirby, and he hooks us up with half a pound of the biggest, juiciest morel mushrooms I've ever seen. He charges us five bucks for what would cost a hundred in New York. I'm curious as to the local customs, and he tells me to soak them in salt water, dry them, bread them, and fry them. And that's just what I intend to do, except for the soaking part. I'm willing to risk an ant or two to maintain full flavor.

I'm not saying this is the best thing you can do with morels, but I am saying it's the best thing you can do with five-dollar-a-pound morels.

FRIED MOREL MUSHROOMS
ROAD INSPIRED AND TESTED

✦ ✦

8 to 10 ounces morel mushrooms
½ cup all-purpose flour
½ cup crushed Ritz crackers
½ teaspoon kosher salt
¼ teaspoon freshly ground black pepper
2 eggs, beaten
Olive oil

Clean the mushrooms and cut them in half lengthwise. Place the flour, crackers, salt, and pepper in a medium bowl and whisk to combine. Place the eggs in a separate bowl.

In 10-inch sauté pan over medium heat, pour in enough oil to completely cover the bottom of the pan and heat until it shimmers. While the oil is heating, toss the mushrooms in the eggs, then dredge them in the flour mixture. Carefully place the mushrooms in the sauté pan and cook until golden brown on all sides, tossing occasionally, 6 to 8 minutes. Transfer to a cooling rack set over a half sheet pan and cool slightly before serving.

YIELD: 4 SERVINGS

This is another case of having so many versions of something on the road that you want to sit down and try to fold them all into one. It's hard, but folding soup always is.

FISH SOUP
ROAD INSPIRED

+ +

½ pound bacon, chopped

2 cups chopped onions

2 carrots, chopped

1 stalk celery, chopped

2 teaspoons kosher salt

½ teaspoon freshly ground black pepper

¼ cup all-purpose flour

1½ pounds catfish chunks

1 quart water

1 cup whole milk

2 tablespoons finely chopped fresh parsley

Place the bacon in a 4- to 5-quart Dutch oven and fry over medium heat until crisp. Remove the bacon from the pot and set aside. Add the onions, carrots, and celery to the pot, along with the salt and pepper, and cook, stirring occasionally, until softened, 10 to 12 minutes. Sprinkle the flour over the vegetables and whisk to combine. Cook, stirring occasionally, for 1 to 2 minutes. Add the fish, the water, and the milk and whisk to combine. Cover and bring to a simmer. Decrease the heat to low and cook at a low simmer until the fish is tender and the soup has thickened slightly, 15 to 20 minutes. Serve topped with the crumbled bacon and the parsley.

YIELD: 4 TO 6 SERVINGS

✦ ✦ ✦ ✦ ✦ ✦ ✦ ✦ ✦

ASPARAGUS FIELD, ILLINOIS 96
1700 HOURS

I see the handmade "Asparagus" sign but can't slow in time. I check my mirrors, U-turn, then roll on the throttle a bit to ease the transition onto the dusty two-track that runs through the field to the railroad track beyond. At the side of the field there is a wooden table. On it sits an old spring-loaded scale and a wood box with a narrow slit cut in it. "$1 a pound" is written on the box. There are also several old kitchen knives, their edges ground down with one of those sharpening wheels they used to put in the back of electric can openers.

I remember U-pick fields from my childhood but I haven't happened across one in quite a while and I've never seen pick-your-own asparagus. We fan out, scouring the acre. The field's been picked over pretty good, and much of what we find is fat, squat second growth, but there's still a good five pounds to be had. There's no trick to picking asparagus. Just stick the knife down into the soil and cut across so you get as much of the tender stalk as possible. Avoid anything more than about eight inches long and steer clear of stalks with any sign of flowering, because they're extremely bitter.

Later that night we camp and steam the asparagus in foil pouches over the fire. J. C. makes a simple dressing of lemons and olive oil and pepper. We eat with our fingers and I do believe it is the best asparagus I've ever eaten.

OPPOSITE: **Cut your own, weigh your own, and drop your money in the box.**

I realize you may not be able to wander into a field to harvest your own asparagus on a lovely spring day. But if you can, obviously it would be a step in the right direction.

STEAMED ASPARAGUS WITH J. C.'S LEMON VINAIGRETTE
ROAD INSPIRED AND TESTED, COURTESY OF J. C. DHIEN

♦ ♦

1 clove garlic
½ teaspoon kosher salt
2 tablespoons freshly squeezed lemon juice
1 tablespoon yellow mustard
Pinch of freshly ground black pepper
¼ cup olive oil
1 pound asparagus, trimmed and rinsed

Place the clove of garlic and the salt in a small bowl and mash together with a fork until a paste is formed. Add the lemon juice, mustard, and pepper and whisk to combine. While continuously whisking, drizzle in the oil until it is well combined and an emulsion forms. Set aside.

Steam the asparagus until tender crisp, 3 to 4 minutes, depending on the size of the asparagus. Drizzle the vinaigrette over the asparagus and serve immediately.

YIELD: 4 SERVINGS

✦ ✦ ✦ ✦ ✦ ✦ ✦ ✦ ✦

DAY TWENTY
JOHN DEERE PAVILION, MOLINE, ILLINOIS
0809 HOURS

From the 1820s to the 1830s, western expansion of this country almost stopped. The problem was the prairie. The soil was and still is dense and sticky, and it bound up and compacted on traditional plows, meaning that for every few feet worked, the poor farmer would have to stop and chisel the compacted dirt off the blade. Many farmers simply gave up and headed back east. The vast center of the country simply could not be farmed, and that made it pretty much useless.

John Deere had the answer. Before he became a blacksmith's apprentice at seventeen, he worked in his father's tailor shop where one of his duties was to sharpen needles by running them through small bags of sand. In his thirties Deere set up a blacksmith shop in Detour, Illinois, where he noticed that he spent the bulk of his time mending plows. He remembered the needles and devised a new plow blade out of high-quality steel that could be polished very smooth. Since it was relatively expensive, he divided the blade into two pieces so that the lower section that did all the cutting could be replaced independently. Deere's plow ripped through the prairie like a razor. Farmers returned and prospered. Westward expansion continued, and the area that was once thought unfarmable became the breadbasket of the world. And that makes John Deere one of the most important characters in the history of food.

The John Deere Pavilion in downtown Moline is a museum dedicated to the evolution of big green machines. Here kerosene-powered tractors from another age stand wheel to tread with state-of-the-art combines, harvesters, and three-story-tall dump trucks. It's an impressive display, to say the least, but if you want to understand how John Deere, the son of a Vermont tailor, changed the world, you really ought to stroll a couple of blocks over to the John Deere Collectors Center, where folks bring their Deere gear from far and wide to be lovingly and skillfully refurbished. I meet the center's manager, Brian Holst, who takes me over to a corner where a platoon of old pull plows rest. Among them stands one of the most important agricultural devices of all time, the Prairie Breaker plow. It looks simple, even childlike. It's not.

If you get a chance to visit Moline, be sure to stop by John Deere. Check out all the cool tractors, harvesters, dump trucks, and combines. Then stop by the gift shop for a hat. Oh, and a block away on River Drive is Froehlich Cakes and Pastries, quite possibly the finest pastry shop in the Midwest. (Who doesn't want a bit of Linzertorte after messing around with farm equipment?)

Foot-powered button lathe, circa 1890.
Courtesy of the Muscatine Art Center.

Early button machines were foot-powered and performed multiple tasks. This lathe cut shell, carved the design on the button, and drilled the holes. Rivpple later adapted motor-powered machines for freshwater mussel shell.

✦ ✦ ✦ ✦ ✦ ✦ ✦ ✦ ✦

MUSCATINE HISTORY AND INDUSTRY CENTER
MUSCATINE, IOWA
1634 HOURS

Muscatine sits on the river—kinda rolls down into it, actually—at a nice wide bend. Walk along the riverbank, poke a little into the ooze, and odds are good you'll come up with a mussel shell drilled with perfectly round holes, like Swiss cheese in a comic book. Congrats: You have yourself a genuine historical artifact.

See, back at the turn of the last century, something like 37 percent of the world's "pearl" buttons were made in this town, all carved from mussel—or, as they were then called, "clam"—shells. Most homes had a primitive mill in the back where

OPPOSITE: **An early blank punch at the Muscatine Button Museum.**
BELOW: **Nothing like a big pile of buttons.**

button blanks were drilled to be sold to a nearby factory for finishing. On the main drag in Muscatine there is a swell museum all about the buttons, and I suggest you drop by and give it a look. Then stroll down West Mississippi Drive to the tiny Clam Shell Diner, which despite the name serves nary a clam. Turns out the mollusks around here make great buttons, but lousy eating.

I step into the Clam Shell and right away something looks familiar. I know I've seen this layout before. Kitchen on one end, L-shaped counter, eight built-in stools. I turn and look over the door and there's the little placard: Valentine Manufacturing Company: Little Chef, serial number 2111. Arthur Valentine started his company in

Wichita, Kansas, in 1947 and specialized in small diners. Not the big, grandiose models you see back east, but petite, practical, affordable diners that he believed would sell well to veterans getting back on their feet after World War II. Valentine's hunch paid off and the company stayed in business through the early 1970s.

The Clam Shell owner, Ann Meeker, fills me in on the history. She tells me that this diner was found in a dump and refurbished before she and her husband bought it in 2005. Everything inside is original, including most of the cooking equipment. I order a Pearl City Dog, which is an interesting concoction. A bun is lined with shredded cheddar, then topped with a deep-fried hot dog. Just think about that a minute. Yeah...me too. Watching the sun sink from the sidewalk outside the Clam Shell I am filled with nostalgia and no small amount of restaurant lust. I want to rip the place off its wee foundations and take it home. Heck, it would probably even fit in the Flame if we moved some stuff around.

OPPOSITE TOP:
I found this shell at the riverside.
OPPOSITE BOTTOM:
The Clam Shell doing brisk afternoon business.
BELOW: Sara Wehage doles out the mustard at the Clam Shell.

✦ ✦ ✦ ✦ ✦ ✦ ✦ ✦ ✦ ✦

KALMES STORE & RESTAURANT, ST. DONATUS, IOWA
1729 HOURS

Half an hour south of Dubuque, Iowa, on Highway 52, sits St. Donatus, a sleepy burg originally settled by Luxembourgians—or would that be Luxembourgers? Not sure. Anyway there isn't so much to see of Luxembourgian culture here, except perhaps at Kalmes Store & Restaurant, which is also a bar and a gas station—the only one in town, near as I can tell. Loud, copyrighted music is playing in the bar, so we decide once again to break out the folding tables and feast on asphalt. It is a beautiful evening, and families are driving into town on their tractors, which is pretty cool. We've been told that Kalmes is the place for that most Iowan of all sandwiches, the pork tenderloin. We order half a dozen, along with some fried chicken livers. We order a bunch of teas, too, which are delivered out to our site not by a waitress but by a lady who's been relaxing with a lovely beverage of her own at the bar. Nice people in Iowa. And a lot of them own motorcycles, by the way. Between six and seven o'clock, fifty or sixty bikes cruise by, pipes blaring. Maybe life here's so quiet they just seem loud.

The chicken livers arrive and right away those of us who love them (meaning me and Ramon) know that something is special about this place. They are the best I've ever had. Crisp and well-breaded, but in no way greasy. The livers are so fresh I actually wonder if the rest of the birds are still alive. The sauce, a spicy seafood-style cocktail sauce, is a welcome change of pace. The sandwiches arrive and are wonderful, but then the owner and head cook, James Kalmes, and his dad, Lawrence, come out with an old mixing bowl full of funny-looking noodles. Hand cut, obviously, and fresh, they appear to be sautéed in butter with salt, pepper, and what looks very much like crumbled-up saltine crackers.

I take a bite and immediately lay claim to the entire bowl. These strange ribbons redefine the buttered noodle experience, and the cracker pieces offer a crisp complement to all that noodly goodness. So simple. So perfect. I beg to be shown how it's done.

OPPOSITE INSET:
Making noodles with Lawrence Kalmes and daughter, Jodi Hingtgen.
BELOW: **Keep away from my Luxembourgian noodles!**

We're invited into the kitchen, and Lawrence calls up his daughter, Jodi, who does most of the noodle making. She's over in about five minutes and happily goes to work mixing eggs, oil, flour, and seasonings. After the dough comes together, Lawrence and Jodi fuss over the texture, adding several handfuls of flour before beginning to roll. Lawrence then breaks out his miraculous pasta roller and cutter, a standard Atlas pasta machine with various cutting heads that can be switched out. The problem with such devices is that you have to roll your pasta, then change to the cutting head and send it back through again. Well, Lawrence had an engineer friend design a wooden box that holds the Atlas (fitted with the rolling head) and the cutting head at an angle underneath. A motor and chain drive links the devices so all you have to do is drop dough in the top. It feeds automatically through the rollers, then feeds down and through the cutters. Genius, plain and simple. If it hadn't have been put together so well I would have opened up the device and taken detailed pictures for the patent application. Alas, it was screwed shut.

After the noodles are rolled and cut, they're usually frozen, broken out as needed, then boiled and sautéed with plenty of butter and crackers. The Kalmeses don't seem to know where this style of noodlery evolved, but I'm thinking it has to be Luxembourg. And to think I'd never given Luxembourgian cuisine a second thought...or a first one, for that matter.

BELOW: A triumph of engineering. This gizmo converts an Atlas hand-powered pasta roller into a motorized roller and cutter. Brilliant.

I've eaten a lot of chicken livers in my day, but these are the best I've ever had. Of course, a long ride on a motorcycle makes everything taste better.

FRIED CHICKEN LIVERS
BASED ON A RECIPE FROM KALMES STORE & RESTAURANT
ST. DONATUS, IOWA

✦ ✦

1 pound chicken livers
1½ cups panko bread crumbs
2 teaspoons Kalmes Steak Seasoning*
Peanut oil

Place enough oil in a 4- to 6-quart cast-iron Dutch oven to come up halfway to the top of the pot. Place over medium-high heat and bring the oil to 350 degrees.

While the oil is heating, clean the livers and rinse them under cool water. In a mixing bowl, combine the bread crumbs and the seasoning and stir to combine. Once the oil has reached 350 degrees, gently add several livers at a time to the pot and fry until golden brown and cooked through, about 1 minute. Remove to a cooling rack set over a half sheet pan to cool for 2 to 3 minutes before serving.

*Kalmes Steak Seasoning contains salt, sugar, paprika, celery seed, onion, chili powder, curry powder, garlic, papain, MSG, and other spice oils. See the list of sources on page 202 to purchase.

YIELD: 4 SERVINGS

BELOW: **Kim Berwanger works the Kalmes griddle.**

Quite possibly the best thing to ever come out of Luxembourg...and that's saying a lot.

NOODLES D-LUXEMBOURG

BASED ON A RECIPE FROM KALMES STORE & RESTAURANT
ST. DONATUS, IOWA

◆ ◆

9 ounces all-purpose flour, plus extra for rolling
3 large eggs
2 teaspoons water
1 teaspoon vegetable oil
½ teaspoon kosher salt
¼ teaspoon freshly ground black pepper
½ teaspoon garlic salt
½ teaspoon celery salt
½ teaspoon onion salt
3 tablespoons unsalted butter
1 cup coarsely crumbled saltine crackers

RIGHT: **Lawrence Kalmes in the kitchen that bears his name.**

Place all of the ingredients except the butter and cracker crumbs in the bowl of a stand mixer with the dough hook attachment. Combine on low speed until the ingredients are well mixed and a dough begins to form. Increase the speed to medium and mix until the dough is no longer sticky, 5 to 6 minutes. Add more flour or water if necessary to create a smooth dough. Shape the dough into a disk, wrap in plastic wrap and refrigerate for 30 minutes.

Remove the disk from the refrigerator and roll out to ¹⁄₁₆ inch thick on a lightly floured surface. Once rolled out, let the dough rest on the counter for 5 minutes. Cut the dough into ¼-inch-wide and 2-inch-long strips and transfer to a half sheet pan lined with parchment paper, separating the noodles as you lay them on the tray.

Bring a 6-quart pot of water to a boil. Gently add the noodles to the pot and cook for 6 to 8 minutes, or until al dente. Meanwhile, place the butter in a 10-inch high-sided sauté pan and melt over medium heat. When the noodles are al dente, transfer them to the sauté pan using a slotted spoon or spider. It is fine if some of the water transfers to the pan as well. Add the crackers and cook, stirring frequently, until the crackers begin to turn golden, 3 to 4 minutes. Serve immediately.

YIELD: 4 TO 6 SERVINGS

The hamburger may be the national sandwich, but the tenderloin sandwich is the Midwest's.

FRIED PORK TENDERLOIN SANDWICH

BASED ON A RECIPE FROM KALMES STORE & RESTAURANT
ST. DONATUS, IOWA

+ +

1 (20- to 24-ounce) pork tenderloin, trimmed
1 tablespoon Kalmes Steak Seasoning*
1 teaspoon freshly ground black pepper
¾ cup panko bread crumbs
Vegetable oil
6 hoagie rolls
Mayonnaise
Lettuce leaves
Tomato slices

Cut the tenderloin into 4-ounce hunks and tenderize each piece until it is ⅓ inch thick. Place the meat in a large bowl and toss with the seasoning and pepper. Add the bread crumbs and toss to combine. Place a griddle over medium-high heat and brush with a little oil. Once the griddle is hot, add the meat and cook until golden brown and cooked through, 3 to 4 minutes per side. Serve on rolls with mayonnaise, lettuce, and tomato.

*Kalmes Steak Seasoning contains salt, sugar, paprika, celery seed, onion, chili powder, curry powder, garlic, papain, MSG, and other spice oils. See the list of sources on page 202 to purchase.

YIELD: 6 SANDWICHES

BELOW: If it's a pork tenderloin sandwich, this must be Iowa. Here served on a hero bun with chopped slaw, potato salad, and a pickle.

Too few people understand a really good sandwich.
JAMES BEARD

MINNESOTA

Bemidji
Lake Itasca
Fargo
Park Rapids
Hibbing
Duluth
Cloquet
Crosby
Superior
Fergus
Falls
Brainerd
Haywa
Morris
Saint Cloud
Elk River
WISCONSIN
Coon Rapids
SAINT PAUL
Minneapolis
Diamond Bluff
Marshall
Red Wing
Stockholm
Old Frontenac
Pepin
Lake City
Nelson
Wabasha
Alma
Fountain City
Rochester
La Crosse
Winona
Trempealeau
Albert Lea 90
Midway
Genoa
De Soto
35
Lansing
Ferryville
MADISON Milwauke
Mason City
Lake
Michigan
Guttenberg
Cassville
esville

**WHISTLE
STOP
CAFE**

MINNESOTA The GOPHER
STATE
OVER 10,000 LAKES
FURTHEST POINT
NORTH IN U.S.
(Before ALASKA)
KEEP MINN.
GREEN
WARROAD
ROSEAU
INTERNATIONAL
FALLS
BAUDETTE
200,000
HUNTERS
PIGEON
RIVER
RAT
Hay Fever
Paradise
Gunflint GRAND
PORTAGE
LOWER
RED LAKE
SUPERIOR NATIONAL
Trail
BEMIDJI
ELY
Source of
Mississippi
Open Pit
Iron Mine
VIRGINIA
GRAND
MARAIS
CASS
LAKE
ITASCA
STATE
PARK
HIBBING
EVELETH
WELL, IT'S
A START!
LUTSEN
TOFTE
SCHROEDER
PARK
RAPIDS
LEECH
LAKE
DEER RIVER
GRAND
RAPIDS
REMER
SILVER BAY
BEAVER BAY
WALKER
LONGVILLE
SCENIC NORTH
TWO
HARBORS
PERHAM
HACKENSACK
EEK!
DULUTH
PINE
RIVER
CROSS
LAKE
Busiest Inland Port
WADENA
NISSWA
AITKIN
WILD
RICE
BATTLE
LAKE
BRAINERD
GARRISON
MILLE
LACS
LAKE
ALEXANDRIA
CAMP RIPLEY

Greetings from
WISCONSI

LUKEFISK EXPRESS

DAY TWENTY-THREE

Great Alma Fishing Float
Alma, Wisconsin
0730 HOURS

THANK YOU

The town of Alma lies along a half-mile stretch of Highway 35, with train tracks and the river flanking it on the west and high, steep bluffs to the east. Lock and dam number 4 is the town's major landmark. The lock is on the Alma side, and on the opposite bank, floating over the dam end and what some say is the best fishing spot on the Mississippi, is the Great Alma Fishing Float.

Owned and operated by Jim and Tim Lodermeier, the float is really a series of interconnected docks with a central hub that contains a few sleeping quarters, a bait and tackle shop, and a small restaurant. If you're on the Alma side of the river you signal the shuttle boat by flipping over a special hinged sign on the small waiting dock. Although we intend to start early for the sake of the fishing, we don't get over and set up until close to 7:30, midday for fishermen. Ten minutes later, we've got lines in the water, though it takes me about six casts to get my minnow five feet from the dock. I've never been any good with a spin rod. Come to think of it, I'm equally inept with a fly rod and a surf rig. Spear fishing?

That I can do. Anyway, sixty seconds go by and Ramon pulls in a nice northern pike, which he immediately follows with a record small-mouth bass and something orange. Half an hour later his lure no longer has to hit the water. Fish are leaping up to it. Fighting over it. Trying to evolve legs so they can crawl up the dock and throw themselves at his feet.

Needless to say, we all hate Ramon. All I've caught is one fairly pathetic bass and so I retire to the "café," where I fall into conversation with Jim and Tim. I see something on the breakfast menu called a "mess." Curious, I ask the guys to make me one and follow them into the galley to marvel at its execution. It's a grocery store on a plate. I thought that since they were already topping it with kraut, some of their float-smoked fish might not be a bad addition. In the end it took three of us to eat one mess. Maybe that's what's wrong with my fishing.

This is the strangest breakfast we encountered on the road and, oddly, the most satisfying. At first glance it seems nothing more than an omelette by Jackson Pollock. It is the sly addition of sauerkraut that makes this memorable, as the tangy cabbage inflects and infuses the whole. I'm proud to say the smoked fish addition was my suggestion.

BOTTOM: Scenes from a fishing float.

MESS
COURTESY OF THE GREAT ALMA FISHING FLOAT
ALMA, WISCONSIN

+ +

1 medium potato, grated
¼ cup diced sausage
¼ cup diced bacon
¼ cup diced ham
2 tablespoons chopped smoked fish (optional)
¼ cup diced onion
½ cup diced green bell pepper
3 large eggs
Pinch of seasoned salt
Pinch of freshly ground black pepper
½ cup shredded Cheddar cheese
½ cup sauerkraut
Toast

Heat a griddle over medium-high heat. Add the potato, sausage, bacon, ham, and fish and fry until browned, 5 to 6 minutes. Add the onion and bell pepper and fry until cooked through, 2 to 3 minutes.

Scramble the eggs on the griddle, then add to the potato mixture and stir to combine. Season with seasoned salt and pepper.

Place the mixture on a plate and top with the cheese.

Heat the sauerkraut on the griddle, then place it over the cheese. Serve the toast on the side.

YIELD: 2 SERVINGS

✦ ✦ ✦ ✦ ✦ ✦ ✦ ✦ ✦

DAY TWENTY-FOUR
RUSSIAN TEA HOUSE, ST. PAUL, MINNESOTA
1403 HOURS

It's cold and windy when we blow into the Twin Cities, and it's almost impossible to keep up with the Great River Road, which twists, turns, vanishes, reappears, and disappears again in the urban landscape. We pull into a parking lot to get our bearings and plan our next move. There's an old gray house in one corner of the lot with a bright red-and-yellow sign reading "Russian Piroshki and Tea House." I have no idea what a piroshki is, but I know that I like Russian-style tea very much. And I know I'm cold. Ergo, we go.

The charming, unfussy Russian Tea House is run by Nick and Linda Alenov, who not only work here but raised three children in this house. Besides Russian tea, the couple serves what they call Russian fast food, which includes a very unbeety borscht (I never knew that borscht means "soup" in Russian and can include a vast number of different ingredients), "lazy" cabbage rolls, which aren't actually rolled at all, and the aforementioned piroshki or Russian hamburger, which is essentially a small loaf of bread containing a spicy beef mixture. I know at first bite that I'm eating the best dish of the entire trip. I immediately inquire about franchise opportunities, but the Alenovs just laugh. Someone notices out the window that there is a sign for a vintage guitar shop on the other side of the building. It's closed now but used to belong to Nick's brother, who was a world-class guitar guy and an avid collector. Whenever big musicians came into town they'd come visit this little guitar shop. The Alenovs remember Dylan being there, and U2 (apparently Bono had the whole menu), George Harrison, and the Stones. Buy a guitar, get a piroshki.

OPPOSITE TOP: Chocolate sweet buns. Thankfully I show restraint.
OPPOSITE BOTTOM: The Alenovs' hand-painted Ukranian-style Easter eggs. They may be cooks, but they sure can paint.
BELOW: Nikolai Alenov with his Russian samovar. The tea blend the Alenovs use contains flower petals and saffron.

NOTEBOOK ENTRY

Russian tea is clever stuff and depends on a properly working samovar. The main body of the samovar is a cylindrical water tank with a small spigot at the bottom and a tube running down through the center. Back in the days before electricity, hot coals were placed in this tube to keep the water hot, as well as the highly concentrated tea in a small pot that sat on top. The idea is that by combining concentrated tea and water one could pour exactly the desired strength of tea.

Although I love their food, what strikes me most about the Alenovs is their chemistry with each other. They've been sealed up in this restaurant with each other every day (the children are gone) for twenty-plus years and yet they seem perfectly smitten with each other. It's lovely to be around them because they radiate a sense of calm that's diffi-cult to find out on the road. They've definitely got a zen thing working. Good for them. And keep the piroshki coming.

I've had a bowl or two of borscht in my time and I've always been under the impression that it had to be extremely beety. I was wrong. I'm very grateful that the Alenovs were willing to share the recipe.

VEGETABLE BORSCHT
COURTESY OF RUSSIAN TEA HOUSE
ST. PAUL, MINNESOTA

✦ ✦

1 cup dry Great Northern beans
1 pound onions, juliennned
1 tablespoon olive oil
2 quarts plus 2 cups water
2½ tablespoons kosher salt
1 pound russet potatoes, cut into ¼-inch cubes
½ pound carrots, peeled and grated
½ pound fresh beets, peeled and grated
½ head cabbage, rinsed and shredded
1 red bell pepper, diced
1 (4-ounce) can pickled beets, with juice
Sour cream
Fresh dill

BELOW: Quite possibly the world's best borscht at the Russian Tea House.

Place the beans in a container, cover with water by 4 to 6 inches, and soak overnight.

Drain and rinse the beans, then place them in a medium saucepan and cover with water by 1 inch. Place over high heat and cook until the beans are tender, about 35 minutes. Drain and set aside.

Place the onions and oil in a small sauté pan over medium-low heat. Cook slowly, stirring occasionally, until caramelized, 45 minutes to 1 hour. Take care not to burn the onions.

Meanwhile, place the 2 quarts plus 2 cups water and the salt in a 6-quart pot and bring to a boil over high heat. Add the potatoes, carrots, fresh beets, and cabbage and bring back to a boil. Boil for 5 minutes. Remove from the heat and add the beans, onions, bell pepper, and pickled beets and stir to combine. Serve topped with sour cream and fresh dill.

YIELD: 6 TO 8 SERVINGS

✦　✦　✦　✦　✦　✦　✦　✦　✦

MICKEY'S DINING CAR, ST. PAUL, MINNESOTA
2237 HOURS

BELOW: Outside Mickey's Dining Car. This is the only real diner that we found on the trip and quite honestly it's the best one I've found, ever. It's utterly authentic in every way: decor, food, ethos, and people. It is perfect.

Motorcycling gets a lot more dangerous at night, so we tend not to stay out much past dark if we don't have to. But by the time we caught wind of Mickey's Dining Car in St. Paul, it's already sunset and there's no way a little lack of daylight is going to stop us. Besides, Mickey's is meant to be approached at night.

Arriving at the diner, it's as though someone parked a time machine next to the street. The modern world, represented by skyscrapers, surrounds the dining car. Warm light spills out of the railway car–like windows and the exterior neon is pumping. Inside, it's like a sitcom cast: the quiet yet wry cook, the ditzy yet charming waitress, the grumpy dishwasher. Even the diner itself is a kind of character, like the Overlook Hotel in *The Shining*, only nice. The owners, Melissa and Gunnar Mattson, have been given a dictate from their dad, who used to run the place: Keep it authentic. The coffee maker they use, for instance, hasn't been manufactured in decades, but they have found folks who find or even make

parts when the need arises. Countertops, stools, everything is either original or period and in working order (except the countertop jukeboxes, which are down at the moment). The food is equally authentic. Nothing goes on the menu that isn't real diner food, and the Mattsons go out of their way to research menu items before making changes or additions.

Although there are four booths at the end of the car, we fill up the stools along the counter and order away. I go for the patty melt, my all-time favorite sandwich. Several others order burgers. J. C. is brave and goes for the liver and onions. Keith Schmitz calmly springs into action, but only after cleaning the flat-top griddle and lubing it liberally with lard. That's right, all the cooking at Mickey's is done with lard. It brings a tear to the eye, don't it? Most of us also order baked beans with bits of meat in it (excellent), and when I notice the chili omelette on the menu something tells me to throw in with that as well. I watch Keith put it together and can't believe my eyes. After blending three eggs for about five minutes, he pours them into a hot pan containing no less than half a stick of butter. With the pan jiggling constantly, the eggs go in and immediately soufflé into a golden pillow. After a few more seconds of jiggling, the pillow is flipped and browned on the other

ABOVE LEFT:
Entering paradise.
ABOVE RIGHT: Lisa,
the fastest-talking
waitress I've ever
encountered.

side. The concoction goes onto a plate and is folded over several pieces of American cheese (not sure how I feel about that one) and is topped with Mickey's chili. Although an emergency text message from my cardiologist begs me not to do it, I dig in...and it is very good indeed. But I show restraint and pass it on for others to try so that I can eat my salad.

RIGHT: The counter-top juke boxes don't work at the moment but maybe someday... BELOW: Lisa guides me through the menu and tells me that whatever I do, I should get the baked beans, which have a fair amount of meat in them.

If I have learned anything about road food it's that when you find a vegetable, eat it—eat all you can—because there's just no telling when you're going to see another one. In this case the vegetable is an interesting cole slaw, which is shredded fine like a slaw but served like a salad, with the dressing on the side. We finish off with wonderful pie and coffee, and I don't want to leave because I've been looking for a place like this to hang out in my whole life. I hope you folks in St. Paul know how lucky you are. If you haven't been by Mickey's lately, make a point to stop by. Have the patty melt or, better yet, the "swing" omelette.

So wrong...and yet so right.

SWING OMELETTE
COURTESY OF MICKEY'S DINING CAR
ST. PAUL, MINNESOTA

+ +

- 3 extra-large eggs, at room temperature
- 3 ounces butter, softened
- 2 slices American cheese
- 1 cup Mickey's Chili (recipe follows)

Place the eggs in a blender and puree on highest speed for 8 minutes. During the last 2 minutes, put the butter in an 8-inch nonstick sauté pan and place over high heat. When the butter is bubbling rapidly, pour the eggs into the pan. Shake the pan in a circular motion. The eggs should fluff while cooking. Once the eggs have set, after 2 to 3 minutes, flip the eggs in the pan and decrease the heat to its lowest setting. Allow the eggs to continue to cook slowly in the pan for another 1 to 2 minutes. Place the cheese on top of the eggs. Fold the omelette out of the pan into a shallow bowl and pour half of the chili into the fold of the omelette. Top the omelette with the other half of the chili and serve.

YIELD: 1 OMELETTE FOR A LARGE, HUNGRY MAN

BELOW: All this puffy goodness is made possible by three minutes in a professional shake blender.

This is darned good chili, but it gets a whole lot better when it's served atop the omelette on page 181.

CHILI

BASED ON A RECIPE FROM MICKEY'S DINING CAR
ST. PAUL, MINNESOTA

✦ ✦

1 tablespoon vegetable oil
1 medium-size yellow onion, chopped
1½ tablespoons kosher salt
1½ tablespoons chili powder
2 teaspoons smoked paprika
1 teaspoon red pepper flakes
2 pounds ground beef
2 cups tomato puree
1 (15-ounce) can red kidney beans
1 cup water

Place the oil in a 6-quart Dutch oven and set over medium heat. Heat the oil until it shimmers, then add the onion, salt, chili powder, paprika, and red pepper flakes and cook until the onion is softened, 6 to 8 minutes. Add the beef and brown thoroughly, stirring occasionally, 5 to 6 minutes. Add the tomato puree, beans, and water and bring to a boil. Reduce the heat to low, cover, and simmer for 25 minutes. Uncover and cook for an additional 5 minutes. Serve as is or use in the Swing Omelette.

YIELD: 2 QUARTS CHILI

✦ ✦ ✦ ✦ ✦ ✦ ✦ ✦ ✦

DAY TWENTY-FIVE
OLSEN FISH COMPANY, MINNEAPOLIS, MINNESOTA
0845 HOURS

I do not intend to leave this part of the country without finding some hard-core Scandana-vian road food, and that means lutefisk—Norwegian for "lye-soaked dried cod." Turns out the country's biggest producer of lutefisk is right in the heart of Minneapolis. Who knew?

Olsen Fish Company is, in fact, right by the river. It's an old family business that has been making lutefisk and pickled herring (among other things) since 1910. Manager Chris Dorff takes me in and shows me the cod, which look and feel just like baseball bats only they're fish without heads. These fish are cured the old-fashioned way, in the wind. When someone puts in a big lutefisk order, these fish go into a lye solution (just like the stuff you make soap out of), which breaks down the protein in the fish, allowing the critter to swell up to larger than its original size and take on a gelatinous consistency. After the lye, the

**BELOW LEFT: Dried cod: good, good for you, and darned fun to play with
BELOW RIGHT: To make lutefisk you've got to have dried cod.**

fish is soaked in several changes of clean water before being packaged. To serve, you simmer the cod in hot water and enjoy. Or not.

Chris shows us the packing line and has a few pounds sealed in plastic just for us. Bear stashes that in a special quarantine section of the Brown Flame's refrigeration unit. We'll deal with it later.

BOTTOM: Alec Garcia, master of lutefisk.

✦ ✦ ✦ ✦ ✦ ✦ ✦ ✦ ✦

BOB'S JAVA HUT, MINNEAPOLIS, MINNESOTA
1650 HOURS

I'm on my own this afternoon. The rest of the bikes, requiring oil changes, have headed to the other side of town to a BMW dealership that Bob knows. Putting around, I see a bunch of bikes parked on a side street by a coffee shop. This in and of itself is not an odd thing, but the mix of bikes intrigues. There's a Harley chopper next to a mid-'70s Moto Guzzi (that primer green always catches the eye) and what I'm pretty sure is a BMW R60. I stop and discover that the owners are all sipping coffee in Bob's Java Hut, perhaps the world's only motorcycle-themed coffee shop. I order an americano and check out the vintage signs and posters. I ask the barista if there's more upstairs. Turns out there's a tattoo parlor up there called Uptown Tattoo and here I am with a couple of hours on my hands and a right arm that's been looking particularly barren. I go up and find Dominic, the owner. I tell him I've really been aching for a skull with crossed knife and fork instead of bones. He

BELOW: My end-of-trip ink. The roman numerals say 2007... I hope.

sketches something out, and in no time I'm in the chair, the electric hum of vibrating needles and that ole familiar ZZZzzzzzz of ink being injected deep into epidermis. Two hours later, I'm sore and behind schedule, racing daylight up the banks of the Rum River and Lake Mille Lacs toward what may be the weirdest inn on the planet.

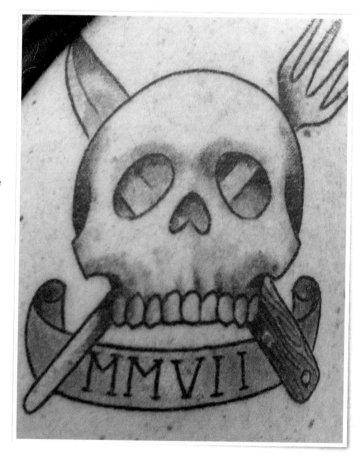

A good traveler has no fixed plans, and is not intent on arriving.
LAO TZU

✦   ✦   ✦   ✦   ✦   ✦   ✦   ✦   ✦

THE NORDIC INN, CROSBY, MINNESOTA
2030 HOURS

OPPOSITE: Just one of the larger-than-life artifacts at the Nordic Inn.
OPPOSITE INSET: Okay, at this point J.C. has traded in his furs for a wig and some Viking chick robes. And it's really working for Bob, who has been on the road way too long.
BELOW: Helga has left the building...and dinner hasn't even come yet.

None of us has brought real cold-weather gear, so camping our last night on the road is out. But that's okay, because Crosby has the Nordic Inn, which we hear is famous. We should have known when they asked us for our sizes that something strange was going on. By the time I arrive at this church-cum-Nordic-stronghold, the rest of my crew has fallen ill with some strange brain fever that has compelled them to dress up like Vikings. There are hats with horns and all sorts of leather wrapping things and swords and in some cases wigs. I am afraid but feel compelled to accept my own costume, which includes a name amulet that reads "Helga." Our host goes by the name Stienarr (pronounced "Styyyy-narrr") and he's assisted by another man and a boy who seems to do much of the work. Everything inside the Nordic Inn is Viking. It puts Epcot to shame. And it's demented. The dinner includes a very strange role-playing show that reminds me of something from a Fellini film. The feast is hearty, with foods that Stienarr and company have researched from lost books of forgotten lore. I especially like the "baby dragon legs." As I record this

it is near midnight and I am about to pass out on a massive pile of furs in my sleeping chamber, which has antlers on the wall and a stone shower in the middle of the room.

RIGHT: **All of Stienarr's appetizers follow a Nordic theme...kinda.**
BELOW: **Luckily we don't have to dress up for breakfast.**

✦ ✦ ✦ ✦ ✦ ✦ ✦ ✦ ✦

DAY TWENTY-SIX
FINAL DAY, NORDIC INN
0700 HOURS

Breakfast is parsley bread from a medieval recipe and a very nice breakfast custard that also has ancient origins. All in all, the Nordic Inn is a blast, but the truth is that you really need wenches. It's just that simple. Bring wives and/or girlfriends and make use of the bedroom in the longboat that juts out over the main hall. If you stay here, make sure you stick around for daylight so you can check out the Viking-themed stained-glass windows. Very nice work.

LEFT: **Breakfast custard with eggs. Good stuff at the Nordic Inn.**

Man cannot discover new oceans unless he has the courage to lose sight of the shore.
ANDRE GIDE

OPPOSITE TOP: **The boat is actually a bedroom.**
OPPOSITE BOTTOM: **Stienarr (aka Richard Schmidthuber) horns us a fond farewell.**

The Nordic Inn is quite possibly the strangest place I've ever been in my life, but dang, this bread is good. It is best served cut into 1½-inch slices, buttered liberally, and toasted on both sides in a skillet until golden brown.

PARSLEY BREAD

BASED ON A RECIPE FROM THE NORDIC INN
CROSBY, MINNESOTA

✦ ✦

1 cup hot water

3 eggs

2 ounces salted butter, at room temperature

19 ounces bread flour (about 4 cups), plus extra for the counter

1 teaspoon kosher salt

1 teaspoon ground cinnamon

1½ ounces currants

3 tablespoons honey

½ cup chopped fresh parsley

1 tablespoon chopped fresh rosemary

1 tablespoon chopped fresh basil

3 teaspoons active-dry yeast

Nonstick spray

In the bowl of a stand mixer with the whisk attachment, combine the hot water, eggs, and butter. Mix on low speed until combined. Switch to a dough hook and add all the remaining ingredients except the nonstick spray. Mix on medium speed for 10 minutes.

Remove the dough from the bowl and place on a lightly floured surface. Knead for 30 seconds, until the dough forms a ball. Lightly grease a large bowl with nonstick spray and place the dough in it, turning once to coat the top. Cover and let the dough rise until doubled in size, 1½ to 2 hours.

Remove the dough from the bowl and place it on a lightly floured surface. Punch down and form into 2 loaves. Place in 2 9-by-5-inch loaf pans sprayed with nonstick spray. Cover and let rise for 1 hour.

Preheat the oven to 350 degrees.

Bake on the middle rack of the oven for 25 minutes. Allow loaves to cool in pan for 5 minutes before turning out onto a cooling rack. Serve warm, cut into 1-inch slices, buttered and toasted on both sides in a skillet until golden-brown.

YIELD: 2 LOAVES

✦ ✦ ✦ ✦ ✦ ✦ ✦ ✦ ✦

HEADWATERS OF THE MISSISSIPPI, ITASCA STATE PARK
1440 HOURS

OPPOSITE: Our
final meal.
BELOW: The official
headwaters of the
Mississippi: twenty
feet wide, one foot
deep.

Two hours on Highway 371 and we hit Itasca State Park. The name Itasca is a combination of two Latin words, veritas and caput, which together mean "true head." The moniker was crafted by explorer Henry Schoolcraft, who was led to the headwaters of the Mississippi by a Chippewa chief (so they say) in the summer of 1832. The spot where the river begins its journey is actually on the north end of Lake Itasca, and it's a very pretty spot indeed, thanks to the efforts of the State of Minnesota, which has invested wisely in this heavily visited area. After a brief meeting with park rangers, we're allowed to ride our bikes down the footpath, over a small bridge, and right up to the river, which is about twelve feet wide and a foot deep. I'm sitting with my feet in it right now. It's very cold and clear, and if I were to drop, say, a cork in it, it would reach the Gulf of Mexico in about ninety days.

Now, if you'll excuse me I have to cook some lutefisk.

WE SIMMERED OUR
LUTEFISK IN MISSISSIPPI
RIVER WATER ON BOBBY'S
JETBOIL RIG FOR EXACTLY
FORTY MINUTES. IT
TASTED LIKE FISH JELL-O,
AND APPARENTLY IF
YOU'RE NORWEGIAN
THAT'S A GOOD THING.
I, HOWEVER, AM NOT,
AND IT WASN'T.

Destination is merely a
byproduct of the journey.
ERIC HANSEN

MISSISSIPPI RIVER FUN
FACTS TO KNOW AND TELL

AVERAGE SPEED: 3 mph

LENGTH: Because it's
constantly changing,
this is a tough one. The
EPA says 2,320 miles,
while the mississip-
pi National River and
Recreation Area says
2,350.

WIDEST POINT: 4 miles,
at Lake Onalaska in
Wisconsin.

DEEPEST POINT: 200
feet, between Governor

Nicholls wharf and
Algiers point, New
orleans.

ELEVATION DROP:
From 1,475 feet
above sea level at
Lake Itasca to 0 at
Head of Passes.

WATERSHED: The
Mississippi drains
41 percent of the
continental United
States.

FOUR DIVISIONS:

HEADWATERS TO ST.
PAUL (head of navi-
gable river): clean,

fresh, winding stream.

UPPER MISSISSIPPI (St.
Paul to St. Louis): pic-
turesque and majestic,
great views from many
limestone bluffs.

MIDDLE MISSISSIPPI (St.
Louis to mouth of Ohio
River): dirty, silty.

THE BIG MUDDY
(Lower Mississippi
from the confluence
with the Ohio at Cairo,
Illinois, to the sea):
slow, gentle, old man
River, often a mile
across.

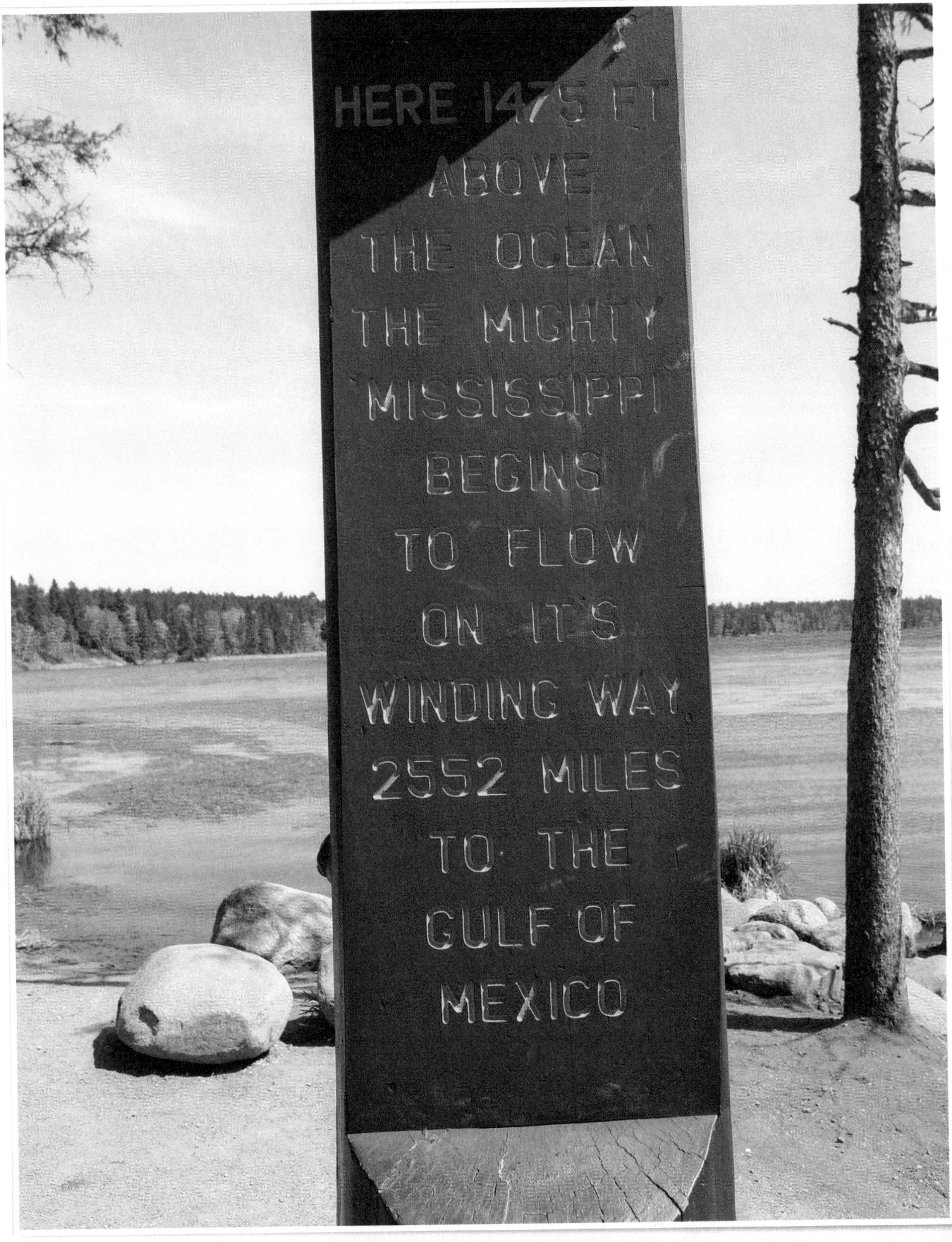

HERE 1475 FT
ABOVE
THE OCEAN
THE MIGHTY
MISSISSIPPI
BEGINS
TO FLOW
ON IT'S
WINDING WAY
2552 MILES
TO THE
GULF OF
MEXICO

✦ ✦ ✦ ✦ ✦ ✦ ✦ ✦ ✦

After burying the lutefisk under the bushes, where it can do no more harm, we brew some coffee, drink it, look at each other and go our separate ways. I ride alone back to Minneapolis, where I spend the night and catch an early plane for Atlanta, where editing duties await. The Brown Flame will pick up my bike and head south. Bob and Bobby will Iron Butt it to Atlanta (that means ride without stopping—it's crazy but kinda fun, too). J.C. will ride west to L.A. Lamar will jet home to South Carolina to meet the baby his wife had while we were on the road. As I turn south I'm struck by how anti-climactic this is. But, truth is, most journeys simply end without fanfare or tickertape. Suddenly, you're just at the place you've been pointed at the whole time and that's that.

But then, arriving isn't the point of the American road trip, is it? The destination is simply the point at which you must stop going forward. I know this, but the knowledge doesn't stop a bit of sadness from seeping in around the edges. Don't get me wrong. I want to go home. I miss my family. But I can't help thinking that there was something that I missed, a turn I should have taken, another flashing "pie" sign I should have heeded.

Next time.

If there is one thing I've learned, it's that the real power of food isn't in its ability to thrill or fill or surprise or please. It's in its ability to connect us to ourselves, to each other, to our heritage, to our land, maybe to our future. Food's a road, and it can lead you to a discovery or two if you let it.

Ride hard, eat hardy, be thankful.

AB

ABOVE: **My last moments with the river.**
OPPOSITE TOP: **Group photo. Expedition complete. Day twenty-six.**
OPPOSITE BELOW: **Looking up river into Lake Itasca.**

LOCATIONS

This resource list will help you find our favorite food stops along the Great River Road. And just in case you want to dine a little deeper we've included here a few bonus locations for your "feasting" pleasure.

DAY 1

Barbeque House
109 Cronin Lane
Venice, LA 70091
P: 985.534.9026
GPS coordinates:
N 29°16.549
W 89°21.438

Jesuit Bend Helicopters
12216 Highway 23
Belle Chasse, LA 70037
P: 504.656.0004
GPS coordinates:
N 29°45.460
W 090°02.264

Luzianne Factory
5601 Chef Menteur Highway
New Orleans, LA 70126
P: 504.241.2213
www.luzianne.com
GPS coordinates:
N 30°00.565
W 090°01.427

Mulate's
201 Julia Street
New Orleans, LA 70130
P: 504.522.1492
www.mulates.com
GPS coordinates:
N 29°56.659
W 090°03.880

DAY 2

Café du Monde
1039 Decatur Street
New Orleans, LA 70116
P: 800-772-2927
www.cafedumonde.com
GPS coordinates: N/A

La Divina Gelateria
3005 Magazine Street
New Orleans, LA 70115
P: 504-342-2634
www.ladivinagelateria.com
GPS coordinates:
N 29°55.500
W 090°05.085

Big Fisherman Seafood
3301 Magazine Street
New Orleans, LA 70115
P: 504.897.9907
www.bigfishermanseafood.com
GPS coordinates:
N 25°55.399
W 090°05.291

Kliebert's Turtle & Alligator Tours
41083 W. Yellow Water Road
Hammond, LA 70403
P: 985.345.3617
www.klieberttours.com
GPS coordinates:
N 30°27.299
W 090°29.103

B&C Seafood Market
2155 Highway 18
Vacherie, LA 70090
P: 225.265.8356
www.bandcseafood.com
GPS coordinates:
N 30°00343
W 090°43.763

DAY 3

Bailey's Andouille & Produce
513 W. Airline Highway
Laplace, LA 70068
P: 985.652.9090
GPS coordinates:
N 30°04.340
W 090°28.345

St. Joseph's Plantation
3535 Highway 18
Vacherie, LA 70090
P: 225.265.4078
www.stjosephplantation.com
GPS coordinates:
N 30°04.41178
W 090°46.42446

DAY 4

The Donut Shop
501 John R. Junkin Drive
Natchez, MS 39120
P: 601.442.2317
GPS coordinates:
N 31°32.34036
W 091°23.77152

Club 601
412 N. Dr. Martin Luther King Jr. Street
Natchez, MS 39120
P: 601.442.5335
GPS coordinates:
N 31°33.644
W 091°23.812

DAY 5

Natchez State Park
230-B Wickliffe Road
Natchez, MS 39120
P: 601.442.2658
GPS coordinates:
N 31°37.119
W 091°13.993

Old Country Store
18801 Highway 61 South
Lorman, MS 39096
P: 601.437.3661
www.theoldcountrystore
lorman.com
GPS coordinates:
N 31°49.240
W 091°03.028

**Biedenharn Candy Co. and
Coca-Cola Museum**
1107 Washington Street
Vicksburg, MS 39183
P: 601.638.6514
www.biedenharn
coca-colamuseum.com
GPS coordinates:
N 32°21.121
W 090°52.082

DAY 6

Jim's Café
314 Washington Avenue
Greenville, MS 38701
P: 662.332.5951
GPS coordinates:
N 33°24.735
W 091°03.71994

Doe's Eat Place
502 Nelson Street
Greenville, MS 38701
P: 662.334.3315
www.doeseatplace.com
GPS coordinates:
N 33°24.939
W 091°03.336

Joe's White Front Café
902 Main Street
Rosedale, MS 38769
P: 662.754.3842
GPS coordinates:
N 33°51.216
W 091°01.656

DAY 7

Ray's Dairy Maid
5322 Highway 49
Barton, AR 72312
P: 870.572.3060
GPS coordinates: N/A

Delta Cultural Center
141 Cherry Street
Helena, AR 72342
P: 870.338.4350
www.deltaculturalcenter.com
GPS coordinates:
N 34°31.37478
W 090°35.1852

DAY 8

Pink Palace Museum
3050 Central Avenue
Memphis, TN 38111
P: 901.320.6362
www.memphismuseums.org
GPS coordinates:
N 35°07.550
W 089°57.555

**Jim Neely's Interstate
Bar-B-Que**
2265 S. 3rd Street
Memphis, TN 38109
P: 901.775.2304
www.jimneelysinterstate
barbecue.com
GPS coordinates:
N 35°05.115
W 090°03.42426

DAY 9

Wiles-Smith Drugs
1635 Union Avenue
Memphis, TN 38104
P: 901.278.6416
GPS coordinates:
N 35°08.142
W 090°0.415

Melanie's Soul Food
1017 N. Watkins Street
Memphis, TN 38107
P: 901.278.0751
GPS coordinates:
N 35°10.05186
W 090°0.6171

DAY 10

Mud Island River Park
125 N. Front Street
Memphis, TN 38103
P: 800.507.6507
www.mudisland.com
GPS coordinates:
N 35°09.017
W 090°03.969

DAY 12

Quapaw Canoe Company
291 Sunflower Avenue
Clarksdale, MS 38614
P: 602.627.4070
www.island63.com
GPS coordinates: N/A

DAY 13

Segar Memorial Park
Chester, IL 62233
P: 618.826.2721
GPS coordinates:
N 37°54.325
W 089°50.018

Alton Visitors Center
200 Piasa Street
Alton, IL 62002
P: 618.465.6676
www.visitalton.com
GPS coordinates:
N 38°53.42622
W 090°11.2065

Fast Eddies's Bon Air
1530 E. 4th Street
Alton, IL 62002
P: 618.462.5532
www.fasteddiesbonair.com
GPS coordinates:
N 38°53.29194
W 090°9.78606

Pie Town Stompin' Ground
2512 College Avenue
Alton, IL 62002
P: 618.465.4779
www.pietownstompin
grounds.com
GPS coordinates:
N 38°54.20622
W 090°8.94612

DAY 15

Prince Pit BBQ
110 Elm Street
Bardwell, KY 42023
P: 270.628.0117
GPS coordinates:
N 36°52.642
W 089°00.848

Fin Inn
1000 W. Main Street
Grafton, IL 62037
P: 618.786.2030
www.fininn.com
GPS coordinates:
N 38°58.1925
W 090°26.81568

DAY 16

Donut Drive-In
6525 Chippewa Street
St. Louis, MO 63109
P: 314.645.7714
GPS coordinates:
N 38°35.516
W 090°18.213

World's Fair Donuts
1904 S. Vandeventer Avenue
St. Louis, MO 63110
P: 314.776.9975
GPS coordinates:
N 38°36.995
W 090°15.681

St. Louis Hills Donut Shop
6917 Hampton Avenue
St. Louis, MO 63109
P: 314.481.6050
GPS coordinates:
N 38°34.399
W 090°17.711

DAY 17

18 Wheeler Restaurant
6723 Highway 6
Taylor, MO 63471
P: 573.769.2848
GPS coordinates:
N 39°55.037
W 091°31.718

DAY 18

Maid-Rite Sandwich Shop
507 N. 12th Street
Quincy, IL 62301
P: 217.222.7527
www.maid-rite.com
GPS coordinates:
N 39°56.276
W 091°23.831

DAY 19

**Baxter's Vineyards/
Carol's Pies**
2010 E. Parley Street
Nauvoo, IL 62354
P: 217.453.2528
www.nauvoowinery.com
GPS coordinates:
N 40°32.538
W 091°31.718

Quality Fisheries
157 Arbor Street
(Highway 96)
Niota, IL 62358
P: 217.448.4241
GPS coordinates:
N 40°37.04178
W 091°17.34426

Asparagus field
Highway 96
Phone: N/A
GPS coordinates: N/A

DAY 20

**John Deere Pavilion
and Collectors Center**
1400 River Drive
Moline, IL 61265
P: 309.765.1000
GPS coordinates:
N 41°30.45282
W 090°31.13934

**Froehlich Cakes
and Pastries**
1524 River Drive
Moline, IL 61265
P: 309.757.0407
GPS coordinates:
N 41°30.48606
W 090°31.03488

**Muscatine History
and Industry Center**
117 W. 2nd Street
Muscatine, IA 52761
P: 563.263.1052
www.muscatinehistory.org
GPS coordinates:
N 41°25.2771
W 091°2.77104

INDEX

A FEW ROAD TIPS

PLAN WITH MAPS, BUT TAKE A GPS

Nothing will give you a better sense of where you are in the big picture than a good paper map. That said, a GPS gives you the freedom to wander without ever getting lost. I find them especially helpful when negotiating the urban landscape, where one-way streets, difficult intersections, and traffic in general can make for treacherous travel. Being able to quickly save a location for future exploration is pretty sweet, and for a motorcyclist, having intel such as time to destination, mileage, and a highly accurate speedometer are very nice indeed. I used BMW's Navigator 3 (no, they don't pay me to say that), which is essentially a Garmin StreetPilot 2820 with extra maps loaded. The sensitive-touch screen is easy to operate even with heavy riding gloves.

PLAN, BUT DON'T OVERPLAN

A good road trip must allow for improvisation. Having a general direction is fine, as is selecting key points of interest. But resist the urge to lay out every moment of the day. I have found random acts of discovery to be the best. And that goes for food, too. Allow yourself the unexpected.

CAMP

It's a beautiful country. Sleep in it from time to time. Cheap, clean, safe campgrounds are everywhere, and I'm especially fond of state sites. You don't need much in the way of gear. Spend decent money on the tent, the bag and the cooking gear, and go cheap on everything else. And don't forget a headlamp. If we'd had those when I was in Scouts I would have made eagle.

(Personal note: When I'm on a motorcycle tour I always have my Big Agnes Seedhouse tent and Lost Ranger bag. My camp stove is by Jetboil. My travel cookware is anodized aluminum.)

SIT STILL

I was perched on a rock outcropping called Buena Vista, which juts over the town of Alma, Wisconsin, about 350 feet above the river. The views to the north and south were biblical, and the sun was just starting to rip up the back end of a heavy squall line. In other words, it was dang pretty. I'd been sitting there half an hour, I guess, when a family of four walked up, stood for a five-count, turned, and left. Don't be them.